100+ Ways to Recharge, De-Stress, and Unmask!

# SELF-CARE
# FOR
# Autistic
# People

## Dr. Megan Anna Neff
Neurodivergent Psychologist and Creator of @Neurodivergent_Insights

Adams Media
New York   London   Toronto   Sydney   New Delhi

**A adams**media

Adams Media
An Imprint of Simon & Schuster, LLC
100 Technology Center Drive
Stoughton, Massachusetts 02072

First Adams Media hardcover edition
March 2024

ADAMS MEDIA and colophon are registered
trademarks of Simon & Schuster, LLC.

Simon & Schuster: Celebrating
100 Years of Publishing in 2024

For information about special discounts for
bulk purchases, please contact Simon &
Schuster Special Sales at 1-866-506-1949
or business@simonandschuster.com.

The Simon & Schuster Speakers Bureau can
bring authors to your live event. For more
information or to book an event, contact the
Simon & Schuster Speakers Bureau at
1-866-248-3049 or visit our website at
www.simonspeakers.com.

Interior design by Julia Jacintho
Images © 123RF/Aleksandr Podoinitcyn

Manufactured in the United States of
America

1  2024

Library of Congress Cataloging-in-
Publication Data
Names: Neff, Megan Anna, 1984– author.
Title: Self-care for Autistic people /
Dr. Megan Anna Neff, Neurodivergent
Psychologist and creator of
@Neurodivergent_Insights.
Description: Stoughton, Massachusetts:
Adams Media, [2024] | Includes index.
Identifiers: LCCN 2023049238 |
ISBN 9781507221938 (hc) |
ISBN 9781507221945 (ebook)
Subjects: LCSH: Autistic people--Mental
health. | Autistic people--Health and
hygiene. | Self-care, Health.
Classification: LCC HV1570.23 .N44 2024
| DDC 616.85/882--dc23/eng/20231109
LC record available at https://lccn.loc.gov/
2023049238

ISBN 978-1-5072-2193-8
ISBN 978-1-5072-2194-5 (ebook)

# Acknowledgments

• • •

This book is a fusion of my special interest energy, years of bewildering adventures as an undiagnosed Autistic human, and the collective wisdom of fellow travelers on this journey.

It all began with my fearless daughter, who led me down the fascinating rabbit trail of autism research. I owe boundless gratitude to the Autistic thinkers, creators, and researchers who have generously shared their knowledge and life experiences, illuminating my path.

A tip of the hat to my ever-patient neurotypical spouse, who constantly loans me his executive functioning and keeps our household afloat while I dive into my hyperfixations, like this project! To my two incredible children, who sprinkle my life with boundless meaning, and my parents, who effortlessly wove accommodations into my world even before we recognized the need for them.

My heartfelt appreciation to my doctoral mentor, Mary Peterson, who recognized the vision of Neurodivergent Insights and encouraged me to forge my own path. I also have deep gratitude to my former therapist, who helped me navigate the depths of my unconscious until we finally unveiled the answer: autism.

I've been fortunate to find neurodivergent-affirming mentors in Donna Henderson, Joel Schwartz, and Finn Gratton. The Autistic community provided a welcoming harbor during the disorienting voyage of late-in-life discovery.

Laura and Rebecca, your unwavering belief in the vision of this project, your boundless curiosity, and your wisdom, have been my guiding lights. Thank you for joining me on this adventure.

# Contents

● ● ●

Preface ............................................. 8

Introduction ...................................... 10

**CHAPTER ONE:**
Cultivating Sensory Safety .......... 12

**CHAPTER TWO:**
Physical Self-Care ...................... 23

*Movement and Regulation*
Manage Your Sensory Needs ...... 24
Understand Your Body's
Responses to Stress ..................... 26
Stimulate Your Vagus Nerve
for Stress Relief ........................... 28
Find Pleasurable Movement ....... 29
Use Breathwork to Relax ............. 30
Unwind Tension in Your Muscles. 32
Support Your Gut Health ............ 34
Use Visualizations
for Sensory Soothing ................... 36

*Sleep*
Create a Healthy Sleep Routine... 38
Put Your Mind to Sleep ............... 40
Create a Sensory Sleep Haven ... 42

*Body Care and Hygiene*
Embrace Adaptive Self-Care
Practices ....................................... 44
Take Care of Personal Hygiene ... 46
Tune Into Your Body's Signals
with a Body Scan ......................... 48
Integrate Body Awareness
Into Daily Activities ..................... 49
Manage Food Challenges:
Executive Function and
Sensory Tips ................................. 50
Supplement with Vitamins .......... 52

**CHAPTER THREE:**
Emotional Self-Care ................... 53

*Autistic Burnout*
Prioritize Rest to Avoid Burnout... 54
Engage In Sensory Detox ............ 55
Identify Signs of Autistic
Burnout ........................................ 56
Drop Unnecessary Demands ...... 58
Find Solace in Familiar Stories.... 59
Clear Emotional Clutter
with a Brain Dump ....................... 60

*Boundaries and Self-Advocacy*
Part Ways with Masking .............. 62
Discover the Power of
Self-Advocacy ............................. 64
Dismantle Stereotypes
about Autism ............................... 66
Manage Hyper-Empathy ............ 68
Curtail the Apology Reflex.......... 70
Break Free from Toxic
Attachments ....................................71

*Emotional Awareness, Literacy,
and Resilience*
Map Out Your Thoughts...............72
Grasp Difficult Emotions..............74
Practice Gratitude..........................76
Repeat Self-Compassion
Statements..................................... 78

*Emotional Regulation*
Practice Affect Labeling...............80
Distinguish Anxiety versus
Sensory Overload......................... 82
Harness the Power
of Effective Worrying................... 84
Uncover Your Raw Spots and
Triggers ......................................... 85
Find Alternatives to Self-Harm... 86
Anchor in the Present Moment... 88
Resist Emotional Avoidance
and Move Toward Acceptance....90

**CHAPTER FOUR:**
Mental Self-Care ......................... 92

*Autistic Identity and Interests*
Celebrate Your Neurodivergent
Identity.......................................... 93
Address Internalized Ableism...... 94
Drop "Functioning" Labels.......... 96
Spend Time Unmasked .................97
Welcome Autistic Stimming ....... 98
Regulate Emotions Through
Movement.....................................100
Identify Your Values .................... 101
Celebrate Your Special
Interests .........................................102

*Self-Advocacy in Mental
Health Care*
Build and Cooperate with
Your Health Care Team .............. 104
Address Co-occurring
Mental Health Conditions......... 106
Find a Neurodivergent-Affirming
Provider ....................................... 108
Explore the Benefits and Drawbacks
of Formal Diagnosis...................... 110

*Autistic Mindset and Well-Being*
Reframe Your Autistic
Childhood Experiences................112
Forgive Yourself ...........................113
Grieve Your Limits........................114
Celebrate Your Authenticity
with an Identity Board ................115

### Mental Health Resilience

Practice Gray Thinking ...............116
Beware of Confirmation Bias ......118
Expose the Stories
Your Brain Is Telling You ..............119
Change Your Relationship
to Your Thoughts .........................120
Identify Cognitive Distortions ...122
Get Unhooked: Eight Ways to
Unhook from Painful Thoughts...124
Practice Mindfulness on the Go...126
Expand Your "Window of
Tolerance"....................................128

### CHAPTER FIVE:
Social Self-Care ......................... 130

### Authentic Relationships

Make Connections
Through Special Interests ............131
Understand the
Double Empathy Problem..........132
Embrace High-Context
Communication...........................134
Connect with Others
Through Story Swapping.............136
Play in Parallel ............................ 137
Join in Autistic Culture...............138
Embrace Object-Based
Conversations ............................ 140

### Interactions with Neurotypicals

Decide Whether to
Tell People You Are Autistic .......142
Craft Scripts for Boundary-
Setting and Transitions............... 144
Practice Context Awareness......146
Navigate Conflict .........................148

### Healthy Relationships

Identify Red Flags and
Green Flags in Friendship...........149
Deal with Rejection Sensitivity... 150
Balance Social Connection
and Alone Time............................151

### Romantic Relationships

Manage Clashing Sensory
Needs ..........................................152
Explore Gender and Sexuality....153
Identify Your Love Language ......154
Navigate Dating Apps and
Websites ......................................156
Plan a Sensory-Friendly Date....158
Find Sensory Accommodations
for Sexual Intimacy ................... 160
Build Emotional Intimacy ...........162
Resolve Conflict in
Relationships...............................164
Embrace an Aromantic
or Asexual Identity ......................166

## CHAPTER SIX
Professional Self-Care...............167

*Workplace Tips*
Selectively Share Your Autistic
Identity with Colleagues.............168
Navigate Context Shifting
in the Workplace .........................170
Document Everything................172
Ditch Perfectionism....................173
Ask for Examples.........................174
Succeed at Job Interviewing.......176
Compare Bottom-Up Thinking
versus Top-Down Thinking .........178
Find a Mentor to Show
You the Ropes.............................180

*Optimal Work Environments*
Manage Overstimulation
at Work.......................................181
Find Accommodations That
Work...........................................182
Reduce Task Switching...............183

*Executive Functioning*
Set SMART Goals.......................184
Create Hyperfocus
Bumper Rails...............................186
Overcome Autistic Inertia..........188

Index .........................................189

# Preface

●  ●  ●

A friend once asked me, "If there was a pill you could take that would make you non-Autistic, would you take it?" I'm not going to lie; I thought about it. It would be nice to be able to be in a room of more than five people and not automatically be sensory overloaded. It would be nice not to brace in pain every time a truck passes by my home office. It would be nice to be able to form (and maintain!) connections with more ease. But I told my friend, "No, I wouldn't take that pill." At the end of the day, I love being Autistic, and... it's hard being Autistic. It's hard navigating a world that wasn't built for me.

I love the creativity and interweaving of my mind. I delight in the dopamine I get from spending hours learning about my special interest. My ability to understand complex things and find patterns enlivens me. My ceaseless curiosity makes life a never-ending wonder.

People with a surface-level understanding of autism often reduce autism to "being socially awkward." However, autism is so much more than social-communication differences. Difficulty with allistic (non-Autistic) communication has certainly caused me some pain, but for me, it certainly isn't the hardest part about being Autistic. *For me, the hardest part about being Autistic is my relationship with my body.*

My body is often a place of too-muchness and not-enoughness—sensory overload, fog, discomfort, and body alienation. Alternatively, many Autistic people stay frozen in the space of perpetual too-muchness and are constantly overwhelmed by the world. To be Autistic is to frequently be intruded upon by the world. The smells, tastes, sounds, and demands for chitchat can feel like constant invasions.

This way of living left me feeling unfulfilled and disconnected. After my autism diagnosis at the age of thirty-seven, following the diagnosis of one of my children, I put my psychological training to work to cultivate a more meaningful, grounded, and value-consistent life. I shifted my focus to working primarily with fellow Autistic adults in my private practice and found connection and support in the online Autistic community. As an Autistic psychologist, I take great pleasure in helping fellow Autistic people develop lives that work for them.

As I became more knowledgeable about my diagnosis, I realized I needed to prioritize self-care. I began to learn how to take care of my body, mind, and spirit in a way that helps me feel grounded, relaxed, and happy. Creating and sharing these education and wellness resources with the neurodivergent community has brought me a sense of purpose and belonging. Thanks to these experiences and learning how to integrate self-care that works for me, I've had less burnout and a deeper connection to others. I hope the ideas in this book help you in your Autistic journey.

You can engage with the ideas in this book in many different ways, depending on your preferences. You might want to skip around to various topics or entries that address needs you have at any given moment, or you can choose to focus on practicing just one exercise for a while. I always advise my clients to be patient with themselves as they learn new things— don't expect perfection immediately (this can be especially difficult for us Autists!). Trying things again and again and learning what works for you and what doesn't is an important part of the process.

What I share in this book has been influenced by my own specific circumstances. I am an Autistic-ADHD individual, which places me in the neurominority category, and I also hold multiple privileged identities, including the ability to speak. While some of this book may have relevance for non-speaking Autistic individuals, I acknowledge that my experience means that this book primarily caters to speaking Autistic individuals without co-occurring intellectual disabilities. In sharing this book from my context, while also holding in mind the complexities of the many intersecting human experiences that I'm aware of, my hope is to provide insights and tools for self-care that resonate with you and that you can apply to your specific context while acknowledging the inherent limits within this text.

Your body is doing amazing things for you every day, and self-care is one way that you can show gratitude and appreciation for all its hard work.

# Introduction

• • •

Many Autistic people experience life in survival mode, trying to avoid and deflect the too-muchness of the world. When you're Autistic, it's as if your nervous system exists on the outside of your body, fully absorbing every single sensory input, social interaction, and piece of information. Although this heightened sensitivity can be a strength—perhaps making you observant, intelligent, and curious—it can also quickly overwhelm your body and mind. It's like your internal battery is always being used, and so it depletes faster than those of your neurotypical peers. That's why you need unique ways to rest and rejuvenate that coordinate with your body's specific preferences. Self-care can act as a protective buffer from the intensity of the world, enabling you to recharge your battery and live a full and engaged life.

Masking, in particular, can drain your battery even faster. Due to the stigma associated with autism, you might mask or repress your natural ways of self-soothing in order to look less Autistic. For example, your body probably wants to avoid eye contact, stim, and/or move to help you ground and regulate. But if you spend your life masking and suppressing this natural instinct, you might experience more sensory overload and become disconnected from your body.

Whether you mask or not, it's important to learn how to take care of yourself in ways that actually reward and nourish your brain, instead of using self-care ideas that are created from a neurotypical lens.

That's why the tips, ideas, and information in *Self-Care for Autistic People* are tailored specifically to address sensory, emotional, relational, and professional challenges so you can feel more aligned with who you are and build a grounded and expansive life.

*Self-Care for Autistic People* includes information on how to work with your sensory and nervous systems, find practices to help you self-advocate, and discover ways to limit burnout. Starting a self-care practice may seem overwhelming, so take your time and focus on the chapters that resonate with you. You can also start by implementing a few practices at a time. Here are just some of the dozens of practices you'll find in this book:

- Manage Your Sensory Needs
- Unwind Tension in Your Muscles
- Support Your Gut Health
- Put Your Mind to Sleep
- Drop Unnecessary Demands
- Identify Red Flags and Green Flags in Friendship

As an Autistic psychologist, I know that fostering a healthy relationship with your autism is key to living a fulfilling life—and self-care can help you do that. You have so much to offer this world, but to do that, you first need to listen to your body, process your emotions, and truly embrace all the wonderful things about yourself. Get ready to build the balanced and joy-filled life you deserve!

# CHAPTER ONE

• • •

# Cultivating Sensory Safety

Self-care is undoubtedly important for everyone. But for Autistic people, it's especially necessary because of the way our bodies interact with the world. Within this chapter, you will explore the significance of self-care for Autistic people and learn how to overcome common obstacles that might hinder your self-care pursuits. This chapter will also go into detail on what is the bedrock of self-care for many Autistic people—sensory self-care. Sensory self-care helps you learn to listen to your body's needs regarding what you see, hear, touch, taste, and smell and then address those needs in a way that works for you.

This chapter prepares you to begin incorporating self-care into your life and establishes the framework for your journey toward holistic well-being. You'll likely find that proactively taking care of yourself feels empowering and enables you to create more situations where you feel calm, focused, and connected.

**An Important Note**

Self-care is not a one-size-fits-all solution. So much of the self-care conversation seems detached from the complexities of real life—after all, what happens when someone doesn't have access to fresh vegetables to make a green smoothie or when the air quality in their neighborhood is so poor that taking a walk would be harmful? Self-care is intricately woven into the fabric of our intersecting identities, which then interact with the surrounding social structures. While I've tried to select self-care activities that can be adapted to various contexts, some of these entries may feel misaligned with your specific circumstances. Systems of oppression that influence BIPOC, disabled people, genderqueer people, and women also need to be addressed to support human thriving. Since these systemic issues are beyond the scope of this book, the entries will focus on the things within your influence that can help foster resilience as you navigate these systems and as we continue to build a more inclusive and safer world for all.

## WHY SELF-CARE IS SO IMPORTANT FOR AUTISTIC PEOPLE

Living in a world that wasn't designed for you can be incredibly exhausting. On a daily basis, you may need to navigate physical, emotional, cognitive, digestive, or other vulnerabilities that many Autistic people experience. Plus, you might find that your specific sensory needs often go unconsidered, your communication and thinking styles are often disregarded, and you are frequently misunderstood. The weight of stigma and negative stereotypes further compounds these daily struggles. On top of that, you have all the "regular" responsibilities and stress that come with being a family member, a romantic partner and/or friend, an employee, and so on.

When you add up all these factors, they can result in you feeling tired, overwhelmed, and/or burned out. You deserve to relax, recharge, and reset your body. That's where *Self-Care for Autistic People* comes in. Taking time to assess how you feel and address your needs is a vital way to restore your energy and tend to your health and overall well-being. Practicing self-care can help you improve your physical health, strengthen your relationships, enjoy more peaceful moments, set boundaries, and achieve goals.

## OVERCOMING THE CHALLENGES OF PRACTICING SELF-CARE

Practicing self-care isn't always easy for Autistic people. Two obstacles might stand in your way when it comes to self-care:

1. Masking

   Masking can pull you away from your authentic experience and make it challenging to connect with your needs and preferences.

2. Interoception difficulties

   Many Autistic people grapple with interoception—the ability to understand your body's internal signals. This further complicates self-care, as you might struggle to accurately gauge your physical and emotional states.

Both of these experiences distance you from your body and its needs—which is the core of self-care.

Self-care starts with self-attunement, which is the practice of tuning into your inner experiences at any given moment. For example, if you're feeling overwhelmed, you might take a step back and ask yourself what specific influence is causing this feeling. What is your body asking for right now? Or, if you're feeling anxious, you may take a pause to notice and name the story your mind is spinning at that moment. For Autistic people, however, the intricacies of masking and the innate challenges with interoception can make self-attunement particularly difficult. Without the ability to assess your internal states, your needs remain obscured, preventing you from addressing them. Complicating matters, you might even dissociate from your body, a protective response stemming from the overwhelming nature of the world around you.

If, like me, you discovered your autism later in life, by the time you realize this about yourself, you may be so disconnected from your body and core needs that you don't even know where to start! This is why, for many Autistic people, self-care starts with rebuilding trust with your body. Your first steps will involve learning to listen to what you need, improving your communication with your body, working through past traumas, and learning to take your needs (and pleasure) seriously. You might not have previously treated your needs with much importance if you are someone who masks. If this is the case, then prioritizing your self-care is actually a profound step toward unmasking and overall well-being. Your body deserves loving care, and you're the best person to provide it. After all, you know yourself better than anyone, so lean on that expertise to put yourself and your needs first.

## WHAT IS SENSORY SELF-CARE?

For most Autistic people, sensory regulation is the fundamental building block of self-care—it's like the foundation of a house. The entire structure will fall apart if the foundation is off. If you lack sensory regulation, all your other systems will be off, and you might experience anxiety, irritability, or meltdowns. You might also struggle to focus when your sensory system goes haywire.

Sensory self-care refers to the intentional practice of managing and meeting your sensory needs. Some common sensory needs include sensory detox, managing sound and smell sensitivity, deep pressure or strong physical sensations, and repetitive movement. When you practice sensory self-care, you'll recognize and respond to these needs in order to create a more balanced and regulated sensory experience. For example, to address the need for deep pressure and sound regulation, you might lie under a weighted blanket with headphones on, listening to your favorite song on repeat. By practicing this type of sensory self-care, you can foster more agency to regulate your emotions, executive functioning, and relationships.

## GET TO KNOW YOUR SENSORY PROFILE

While you have more than five senses, there are typically the "big five" that come to mind when we talk about sensory sensitivities: taste, smell, touch, sound, and sight. These five senses have a powerful influence over how you experience any given moment.

The first step in prioritizing sensory self-care is getting to know what bothers you (your triggers) and exactly what your ideal sensory experience entails (your preferences). Collecting this information may sound simple, but it can be a bit of a complex task for many Autistic people because:

1. You may have paradoxical or conflicting sensory experiences.

2. Many Autistic people struggle with body awareness, so you may have a hard time decoding what your sensory experience even is.

If this task is challenging for you at first, know that you'll get better at it as you practice. Getting clarity about your sensory triggers and preferences in each of these five domains can equip you to accommodate your needs and cultivate an ideal sensory environment. (See the Manage Your Sensory Needs entry in Chapter 2 for more ideas on managing your five traditional senses.)

## Identifying Your Sensory Triggers

Sensory triggers are the things that grate on your nervous system and cause sensory overload, such as loud or unexpected noises, bright lights, certain textures, unexpected touches, and strong smells.

If you struggle with body awareness, you may not even know when or why you're feeling sensory overload; you might simply register that you feel bad or have a headache. This is a problem because if you aren't comprehending that your sensory system is overwhelmed, then you won't take steps to regulate yourself! It's as if odorless poison were slowly creeping in and you didn't realize it. Learning to identify your sensory triggers helps you be more proactive in removing yourself from sensory-triggering situations if possible and addressing overload that does arise if not.

Working to identify your specific triggers is sort of like being a detective. For example, the next time you have a headache or a wave of anxiety (note that sensory overload may feel like anxiety), do a quick scan of your body and surroundings: Is there anything bothersome about your environment? Are you under a bright light? Is there a strong smell near you?

Again, you are the expert on yourself, so get curious and use that agency to improve your experiences. Discovering your sensory triggers can take some time and attention, but it's well worth the effort. Here are some ways to begin identifying your triggers:

- **Keep a sensory-trigger journal:** Jot down how you feel throughout the day and what experiences cause discomfort or distress.

- **Conduct a mindful environment scan:** Do a scan of your environment whenever you have a wave of discomfort to see if you can identify potential triggers.

- **Notice muscle tension:** Pay attention when your body is clenching or bracing, and note what is happening around you at that time.

- **Seek professional support:** Consider working with a trained professional, like an occupational therapist, who can guide you through identifying your sensory triggers and developing strategies to manage them.

Knowing your sensory triggers will help you manage your environment and self-advocate for spaces that work for you. For example, when you enter a restaurant, you might say something like, "I have light sensitivities. Is it okay if we sit in that corner rather than under this light?" Taking control of your experiences in this way can empower you and help build self-advocacy confidence—which are also forms of self-care!

### Identifying Your Sensory Preferences

Many Autistic people find it easier to identify sensory triggers than sensory preferences. However, sensory preferences are just as important as sensory triggers. Your sensory preferences are what help you feel calm in your surroundings and soothe you when you're upset. Creating a soothing sensory environment helps you focus more effectively, stay grounded, and engage with people around you.

Sensory preferences will vary a great deal from person to person. Someone who is highly sensitive to visual input may enjoy dim lighting in a clean and organized environment with no visual clutter. On the other hand, someone who is a visual seeker may enjoy disco lights, LED lights, spinners, and other visually stimulating elements. There are no right or wrong answers here; you decide what works best for you.

There are a variety of ways to explore your sensory preferences. You can:

- **Cultivate self-awareness:** Take time to reflect on your experiences and how you respond to different sensory stimuli. Notice how certain sounds, textures, smells, tastes, and visual stimuli affect your mood, energy levels, and overall well-being.

- **Keep a sensory journal:** Create a journal where you document your observations and reflections on your sensory experiences.

- **Get feedback:** Ask trusted friends and family members how they think you respond to different environments.

- **Use sensory checklists:** A sensory checklist is a comprehensive list of sensory options, usually categorized by the different senses. You can find several free sensory-preference checklists online (simply search "sensory-preference checklist," or go to my website, NeurodivergentInsights.com, where I have several free sensory checklists).

When you get a handle on what your sensory preferences are, you can make small changes to your surroundings to create a more peaceful, calming environment; be better equipped to advocate for your sensory needs; and know what soothes you when you are upset or experiencing sensory dysregulation. These are all ways of practicing self-care as well!

## UNDERSTANDING BALANCE AND MOVEMENT

Sensory self-care goes beyond your five senses and also includes three hidden or invisible sensory systems: proprioception, the vestibular system, and interoception. Let's look at each one in more detail.

### Understanding Proprioception

Proprioception refers to your ability to know where your body is in space without consciously thinking about it. Proprioception receptors are located in muscles and joints and provide information about where your body parts are and how much pressure to apply. Proprioceptive "under-responders" crave proprioceptive input and likely enjoy the experiences of pressure, weight, constrictive clothing, intense movement, and more. Proprioceptive "avoiders" are sensitive to the slightest of touches and may be accused of overreacting when someone brushes up against them. Discovering tolerable methods to incorporate proprioceptive input into your sensory routine, while also advocating for your body's boundaries, is key when you are a proprioceptive avoider.

### Understanding Your Vestibular System

Your vestibular system helps you coordinate balance and movement. In your inner ear, there are receptors that not only help you tell how fast you're moving and in which direction but also assist in deciding how fast to move and in what direction. If you're a vestibular system "under-responder," you seek out more movement and vestibular stimulation (things like swinging, rocking, bouncing, and jumping). Over-responders, on the other hand, experience this stimulation to a high degree and experience motion sickness more easily. Things like riding in cars, in elevators, and on escalators and even walking up the stairs can bring on discomfort. If that's your experience, you will benefit from taking movement slow and not intentionally engaging in activities designed to make you dizzy (don't be peer pressured into spinning teacup rides!).

### Understanding Interoception

Finally, interoception has to do with accurately perceiving what is happening *inside* your body (like your heartbeat, hunger, and emotions). If you have heightened interoception awareness, you likely feel everything at max volume but may struggle to differentiate what is what (for example, what is anxiety versus hunger). If you have lower interoception awareness, you likely struggle to experience things like thirst, hunger, the urge to use the bathroom, and emotions. If you struggle with interoception, putting your body's basic needs on a schedule is vital because you may not receive the signals when your body needs something.

## COPING WITH SENSORY CHALLENGES

Navigating these sensory challenges is an important first step in your self-care practice. The following ideas will give you a general framework for managing your sensory needs so you can begin to think about an even wider range of self-care options. These suggestions will empower you to identify and embrace your needs and celebrate your ability to address them.

### Create a Sensory Safety Plan

After you identify your sensory triggers and preferences, you can write a safety plan that captures your key findings. Developing a personalized sensory safety plan can help you anticipate and manage potential triggers. Write down calming strategies, safe spaces, and tools that comfort you. Additionally, brainstorm an exit strategy when you must be in an overwhelming sensory environment. Having this information written down ahead of time will allow you to navigate challenging sensory situations with more ease.

### Understand and Cope with Meltdowns

Meltdowns occur when sensory overload becomes too overwhelming and your sensory system, well, melts down. During a meltdown, it may feel like all the sensory signals are screaming at you, as if you have lost control of your body and actions. Meltdowns can be disorienting, anxiety inducing, embarrassing, and exhausting! One of the goals of your self-care practice will be to avoid or minimize the frequency of these high-stress situations by spotting your triggers.

Recognizing the early signs of a meltdown and having a plan in place so that you can quickly implement self-soothing techniques can help you manage and recover from these intense experiences. Additionally, practicing self-care in the aftermath of a meltdown is important, as many Autistic people experience a lot of shame around meltdowns.

### Understand and Cope with Shutdowns

Shutdowns are physically similar to meltdowns, but they look like the complete opposite on the outside. A shutdown is when a person has experienced sensory overload and their body responds by dissociating and shutting down. Shutdowns are tricky because, to the outsider, you likely look calm. During a shutdown, your body is taking in the sensory stress and freezing it—but the situation is still very stressful. It's very important to realize that your body is in a state of stress and your body needs to complete the stress cycle and release the stress when it is safe to do so. The ideas throughout this book will help you release this pent-up stress energy and return to sensory safety.

### Embrace Your Sensory Needs

One of the most effective things you can do to address sensory challenges is to accept and love yourself just as you are. Simply embracing your sensory needs is a crucial and powerful act of self-care. This involves:

- Getting curious about your sensory experience.
- Acknowledging and accepting your sensory preferences.
- Adjusting to your surroundings to create a sensory-friendly environment.

You are always worthy of love and care; recognizing and tending to your sensory needs is one way that you can show your body and mind that affection.

## INCORPORATING OTHER TYPES OF SELF-CARE

Sensory self-care is the bedrock upon which other self-care practices are built—you'll want to keep practicing these skills even as you explore other important types of self-care. In fact, you'll find that you frequently refer back to your sensory needs in each of the other categories covered in this book:

- **Physical self-care:** This category includes anything that helps you care for your body. For example, you can learn to build good sleep habits and explore strategies to work with your sensitive nervous system so you feel more regulated and grounded in your body.

- **Emotional self-care:** This category involves activities aimed at developing emotional awareness and resilience. For instance, you can expand your emotional awareness and literacy, enabling you to better identify and process your emotions.

- **Mental self-care:** Mental self-care includes practices that support your mental health and wellness. This can include things like identifying and aligning with your values, which can bring a sense of clarity and purpose to your life, and embracing mindfulness, which strengthens your ability to attune to yourself in any given moment.

- **Social self-care:** Social self-care encompasses techniques that assist you in navigating social situations with care. Learning how to establish and nurture meaningful relationships, as well as understanding and embracing Autistic communication patterns, can pave the way for more genuine and valuable connections.

- **Professional self-care:** This topic covers how to nurture your professional self and thrive in your workplace. For example, you can find a helpful mentor and seek accommodations for enhanced workplace comfort.

Autistic people often face barriers, stigmas, and difficulties in each of these areas, making intentional self-care practices that much more important. As you read the ideas in this book, you will find ways to recharge your battery, cultivate resilience, and connect with your authentic self. When you take care of yourself, you'll embrace and appreciate your true identity and more fully engage with the world. Let *Self-Care for Autistic People* be your guide as you walk this path toward strength, harmony, and joy.

# CHAPTER TWO

• • •

# Physical Self-Care

Have you ever thought, "I wish I could be a mind in a jar"? Many Autistic people share this sentiment because having a body is just so much work! If you struggle with the more embodied aspects of being human, that can impact your physical self-care.

Complicating matters, when you don't feel good in your body, some of the more challenging parts of being Autistic become heightened. For example, your need for routine can be intensified when your body feels unwell. And interacting with others can go from manageable to unbearable! Physical discomfort hampers executive functioning, making planning, organizing, and carrying out daily tasks more difficult.

There are valid reasons why physical self-care can be challenging for Autistic people. Sensory issues can make physical self-care overwhelming. Low body awareness can create difficulties, and executive functioning struggles make it harder to initiate and maintain consistent self-care routines. Regardless of this complex relationship with your body, you *are* capable of caring for your body, one action at a time.

In this chapter, you will find activities designed to help you discover what types of physical self-care work best for you. You might want to enjoy movement, reset your nervous system, prioritize healthy sleep habits, or explore exercises that enhance body awareness. The activities in this chapter are broken down into categories—Movement and Regulation, Sleep, and Body Care and Hygiene—so you can easily find ideas that will help your body thrive. To avoid feeling overwhelmed, try to implement just one or two activities that resonate with you and be gentle with yourself as you incorporate new self-care into your life.

# Manage Your Sensory Needs
## Movement and Regulation

Navigating the sensory landscape as an Autistic person presents unique challenges. That's because around 90 percent of Autistic people grapple with sensory-processing differences and can experience either sensory hypersensitivity or hyposensitivity. Sensory hypersensitivity may lead to avoidant behaviors, like evading bright lights or loud sounds, while hyposensitivity results in dulled perceptions. Some Autistic people are also sensory seekers, meaning that they pursue dynamic visuals or crunchy textures.

Understanding and managing your senses is a form of self-care that allows you to be observant of what works for you, then empower yourself to shape your sensory experiences accordingly. Let's explore how to manage the five core senses.

### TASTE: Balancing Preferences and Sensitivities

Autistic people often have distinct taste preferences and sensitivities. Here are some common situations and ideas for handling them:

- If you find comfort in a select group of "safe foods," especially during stressful times or transitions, embrace that habit as a form of self-care. Eating these safe foods can provide stability when your sensory world feels overwhelming.

- If you're a sensory seeker in the taste realm, try spicy and crunchy foods to excite your taste buds.

- If you are hyposensitive to taste, be aware of potential risks, like not recognizing spoiled food. To ensure freshness, regularly check expiration dates and consider implementing a color-coded or visual system in your fridge, especially if you frequently consume leftovers.

## SMELL: Creating a Soothing Olfactory Environment

Your sense of smell can be a double-edged sword, as it can either overwhelm you or provide a source of joy. If you're sensitive to smells, try eliminating toxins and chemicals from your living space to reduce discomfort and minimize migraine triggers. If you live with others, feel free to mention how smells affect you and see if everyone is on board with sensory-friendly options. On the other hand, sensory-seeking individuals might relish scented products.

If you are a hyposensitive smeller, being aware of potential dulled sensitivity to smells is essential for safety as you will have more difficulty identifying toxins in the air. Consider installing specialized air-quality detectors or alarms in your living space, which can provide an extra layer of safety by alerting you to any harmful substances in the environment.

## TOUCH: Navigating Preferences and Comfort

Clothing choices can greatly impact your sensory experience. Whether you prefer constriction or a loose fit, opt for sensory-friendly clothing that you find comfortable. Depending on your preference, either style can act as a buffer against sensory overload.

## SIGHT: Embracing Visual Comfort

Visual stimuli can be both captivating and overwhelming. You can create a peaceful sanctuary by identifying visual inputs that soothe your senses and incorporating them into your environment. If you need to manage visual overload, try reducing visual clutter, using sunglasses, or dimming lights.

## SOUND: Striking a Harmonious Auditory Balance

Sound sensitivities can disrupt your equilibrium. Make a list of sounds that bring you comfort so you can refer to it when you need to be soothed. Consider using tools like noise-canceling headphones or sound machines to regulate your auditory experiences.

# Understand Your Body's Responses to Stress
## *Movement and Regulation*

Do you feel stressed by things that seem minor to others? Do you notice your heart racing and a feeling of panic when too much information comes at you? Do you ever feel overcome with a wave of fatigue or feel like life isn't real, almost as if you were in a dream? These are all signs that your body is flipping into a stressed state. While everyone feels stressed at one time or another, these experiences happen more often for Autistic people. Our nervous systems tend to be less flexible than others', which means we become stressed more easily. Because of your more sensitive nervous system, you likely spend more time in stressed body states, such as fight-or-flight or shutdown mode. Learning to nurture your nervous system is a big part of caring for your body.

When your nervous system is stressed, it goes one of two places—it either revs up and goes into fight-or-flight mode, mobilizing you for action, or it goes into a protective shutdown to reduce incoming sensory input (in other words, it sort of immobilizes you, a state known as freeze). While stress is typically associated with revving up, Autistic people appear to be more prone than the average person to respond to stress by going into shutdown mode. This means you may be experiencing stress, but it's not registering (to you or the people around you!).

When you learn to track and map your nervous system's response, you can better address your body's needs from moment to moment. Here's a rundown of what you might experience in each stressed state, and how to then provide your body with the care and support it needs.

### Fight-or-Flight State

This state can feel like a surge of energy, or intense emotions. Examples include feeling restless, agitated, anxious, and overwhelmed. During the fight-or-flight response, engaging in activities that release excess energy or promote relaxation helps complete the stress cycle. You could try some vigorous exercise, deep breathing, or progressive muscle relaxation (see the Unwind Tension in Your Muscles entry in this chapter for detailed instructions) or find a safe outlet for emotional expression.

### Freeze or Fawn State

In this state, you might feel emotionally numb, fatigued, disconnected, or dissociated. It can lead you to feeling immobilized or stuck or overly compliant in social situations. In freeze-fawn mode, you are likely to seek to appease others and have difficulty setting boundaries or asserting yourself. In this context, appeasing others is a way that you might unconsciously protect yourself from threat.

When experiencing freeze-fawn mode, your body benefits from gentle and soothing activities to help regulate the nervous system, such as taking a warm bath, gently swaying, or practicing grounding techniques, like focusing on a specific sensory input (for example, you can hold a cup of tea and concentrate on the warmth emanating from it, or you can apply a heating pad to your body and focus on the sensation of heat spreading).

# Stimulate Your Vagus Nerve for Stress Relief

## Movement and Regulation

Many Autistic people have what I call a "rigid" nervous system, which means our nervous systems don't adapt as easily to incoming stressors and we more easily flip into stressed states (think fight-or-flight and freeze-fawn). This is measured through something called vagal tone, which is associated with the vagus nerve.

The vagus nerve, also called the "wandering nerve" because it interweaves throughout your major organs, influences your heart rate, breathing, and more. It is the core nerve responsible for relaxation. Having a high vagal tone allows you to adapt flexibly to your environment and handle incoming stressors without flipping into a stressed state.

Autistic people often have low vagal tone—meaning you might struggle to adapt to incoming stressors. This all happens on an automatic level. So when your nervous system has a response, it's not because you're weak; it's an involuntary response, much like a sneeze or cough. The good news is that you can improve your vagal tone.

One way to strengthen the vagus nerve is by activating the muscles connected to your vocal cords. Activities like chanting, humming, gargling, and singing use these muscles, stimulating the vagus nerve. These practices help trigger your relaxation response while simultaneously increasing your vagal tone. Try out a few different methods and take note of how you feel. You can build time into your day to chant, hum, gargle, or sing, or simply do them when you're feeling overwhelmed to help reduce stress.

# Find Pleasurable Movement
## Movement and Regulation

Movement does wonders for your body and mind. It improves heart health, boosts your mood, reduces stress and anxiety, helps your brain operate more smoothly, releases endorphins (the "happy" hormone), and promotes better sleep, among other benefits.

Some Autistic people struggle to prioritize movement, perhaps because coordination and balance may not come easily. This can make traditional exercise routines feel intimidating and overwhelming. Furthermore, traditional exercise opportunities, like in gyms or on organized sports teams, can be sensory nightmares, and it's easy to feel anxious about knowing the social norms of new places.

You might, therefore, find it more helpful to prioritize *pleasurable movement* over traditional forms of exercise. By discovering movements you genuinely enjoy, you can create a soothing and gratifying experience that you are likelier to stick with.

Many Autistic people find repetitive movements like swimming, Rollerblading, skating, running, and walking to be particularly soothing. Pairing such an activity with a stim song can be especially rewarding! You can even think outside the box and try stim dancing or a repetitive circuit-training routine.

Whether it's swimming, dancing, walking, or any other activity that resonates with you, make it a priority to figure out what types of movements make you feel good. These activities provide a sense of rhythm and flow that can calm your nervous system while also providing health benefits.

# Use Breathwork to Relax
## *Movement and Regulation*

Breathwork can be an incredibly useful tool for helping you reset your nervous system. This self-care practice provides a way to interrupt the stress cycle and help your nervous system return to a nonstressed state. It seems simple, but it's really powerful—by intentionally connecting with your breath, you can gently guide your nervous system back to a state of balance.

Breathwork is a practice that involves conscious control and manipulation of your breathing patterns. It is based on the understanding that your breath is intricately connected to your nervous system, so by altering your breathing, you can influence your nervous system's state, which in turn influences your emotions. This ancient practice, simple yet profound, empowers you to cultivate a sense of inner calm by activating your body's built-in relaxation response. Something as simple as taking a deep breath activates the vagus nerve, which helps you relax!

You may initially find breathwork challenging due to difficulties with body awareness or coordination. However, with patience, adaptation, and visual techniques, it can become an invaluable nervous system reset tool.

**To try out breathwork:**

- Find a comfortable space where you can focus on your breath. You may choose to lie down or sit comfortably.

- Allow your body to settle, and bring your attention to the natural flow of your breath.

- Intentionally slow down your breathing pattern, with a particular focus on lengthening your exhale.

- Notice the gentle rise and fall of your abdomen (pay attention to whether or not your stomach rises and falls or if just your chest does, as many people initially struggle to get the breath all the way into their diaphragm).

- If you're struggling to get the breath into your belly, place your hand on your stomach, or if lying down, you can place a small stuffie or book on your stomach. Try to get your hand (or the object) to rise and fall with the breath. This visual feedback is helpful when first learning.

- You can also count as a way to make the practice more concrete.

**To use counted breathwork:**

1. Inhale through your nose slowly while you slowly count to four.

2. Hold your breath for one second

3. Slowly exhale through your mouth while you count to six (slowing down the exhale is particularly helpful for activating the vagus nerve).

4. Hold for one second, then repeat.

These breathwork activities can help reduce anxiety, improve sleep, improve vagal tone, enhance focus and attention, and increase overall well-being. It's pretty amazing that you can do all that by simply manipulating your breathing patterns! If you're just starting out, be gentle with yourself. Like any skill, it may take time to develop, especially if you struggle with body awareness. Trust your intuition and feel free to modify and adapt breathwork to best suit you.

# Unwind Tension in Your Muscles
## Movement and Regulation

In the hustle and bustle of daily life, tension builds up in your muscles, leading to physical discomfort and added stress on your nervous system. Progressive muscle relaxation (also known as "tense and release") is a powerful self-care practice that can help you release this tension and activate your body's natural relaxation response.

Progressive muscle relaxation is rooted in the understanding that when your muscles are relaxed, your mind relaxes too. You can cultivate this sense of deep calm by systematically tensing and releasing different muscle groups. Relaxing your muscles activates the parasympathetic nervous system (which then activates your built-in relaxation response). This process shifts you from feeling agitated to feeling calm.

To engage in progressive muscle relaxation:

- Take a few deep breaths, allowing your body and mind to settle.

- Clench and tense the muscles in your feet for 3–5 seconds.

- Focus your attention on the sensation of tension in those muscles. Once you have experienced the tension, release it completely, allowing the muscles to relax and soften.

- Pay special attention to the contrasting sensations of tension and relaxation. Notice the sensation as the muscles let go of their tightness.

- Next, move onto your calves, then continue upward to each major muscle group. Tense for 3–5 seconds and release. Continue this process of tensing and relaxing different muscle groups throughout your body, working your way up to your head.

- Breathe deeply as you release tension, allowing your exhalation to carry away any residual tension. Visualize the tension melting away from your body with each release.

Research has shown that regular practice of progressive muscle relaxation offers numerous benefits. It can reduce muscle tension, decrease physical discomfort, improve sleep quality, decrease anxiety and stress levels, and enhance overall relaxation and well-being. By incorporating progressive muscle relaxation into your self-care practice, you empower yourself to unwind tension, foster a greater mind-body connection, and support your body's natural ability to regulate and find balance.

Progressive muscle relaxation has added benefits for people with sensory sensitivities or difficulties with body awareness. As you consciously focus on each muscle group and the sensations within, you strengthen your body awareness and deepen your connection to your physical self.

Like most things, progressive muscle relaxation is a skill that requires a bit of practice! Consider exploring guided progressive muscle relaxation audios or videos to have a framework the first few times you do it. By incorporating progressive muscle relaxation into your self-care routine, you unlock a powerful tool for unwinding tension while nurturing your nervous system.

# Support Your Gut Health
## *Movement and Regulation*

In recent years, researchers have learned a lot about the connection between the gut and the brain. The condition of your gut plays a pivotal role in influencing not only your mental health but also your overall physical well-being. Poor gut health can contribute to inflammation and trouble with cognitive functioning. Autistic people are more susceptible to experiencing gut-related issues, so here are some practices that can support your gut health:

### Mindful Eating
- Pay attention to what you eat and how it makes you feel.
- Consider incorporating gut-friendly elements like probiotics and fiber-rich foods into your diet, but be mindful of conditions like leaky gut or small intestinal bacterial overgrowth (SIBO) when incorporating probiotic-rich foods.

### Hydration
- Stay hydrated by drinking an adequate amount of water throughout the day. Proper hydration supports digestion and overall gut function.

### Stress Management
- Stress takes a toll on your gut! Explore stress-reducing techniques such as deep breathing, progressive muscle relaxation, and engaging in activities that bring you joy and relaxation.

### Reducing Alcohol Use
- Alcohol can have negative impacts on your gut. Consider eliminating or reducing alcohol to improve gut health.

### Working with a Holistic Provider

- Working with a functional medicine provider, naturopath, or holistic provider who understands "All the Things" (a term describing the interconnectedness of health systems and vulnerabilities, as coined by Dr. Mel Houser, an Autistic physician) and autism can help you create a personalized plan to support your gut health.

Supporting your gut health is such a vital part of your holistic well-being.

# Use Visualizations for Sensory Soothing

## Movement and Regulation

Visualizations allow you to immerse yourself in pleasant, imagined places so you can melt into moments of safety, comfort, connection, sensory pleasure, and tranquility. By harnessing the power of your imagination, you can create a sacred sensory space that calms your nervous system and provides a sensory haven. Sensory visualizations are a powerful self-care practice because they offer a respite anytime and anywhere amid life's demands. Plus, they are yet another powerful relaxation exercise to help regulate your nervous system.

**Here's how to try it:**

- Find a physical space that's as free of distractions as possible. Then close your eyes and think of a location that holds personal significance for you—this could be a treasured memory from a past visit, an image that has resonated with you, or a setting depicted in a beloved book or movie.

- Once you have the place in mind, go through each of your five primary senses, imagining what you would experience:

  1. Start by **visualizing** what you would see in this place. Take in the colors, shapes, and scenery surrounding you.

  2. Next, focus on the **scents** that would fill the air. Breathe in deeply and imagine the fragrances that waft through this space.

  3. Move on to the sense of **taste**. Imagine the subtle flavors that linger in the air or foods you might encounter in this environment, such as the sweetness of a gentle breeze or a comforting beverage.

4. Shift your attention to **touch**. Bring to mind textures and sensations you would encounter. Feel the softness of a blanket against your skin or the coolness of water on your fingertips. Allow these tactile sensations to deepen your sense of connection to the place.

5. Finally, focus on the **sounds** that surround you. Tune into the ambient or natural background sounds filling this space.

• Be present with each layer of sensory experience, savoring the sensations that arise. There is no right or wrong way to experience a sensory visualization. Allow your imagination to guide you, and embrace the sensory details that resonate with you.

Incorporating sensory visualizations into your self-care or sleep routine can provide moments of respite, rejuvenation, and connection to sacred spaces. Cultivating this safe sensory space in your mind creates a soothing experience, allowing you to unwind and find relief from any overwhelming feelings you face.

Note: Some Autistic people have aphantasia, which means they are unable to visualize images in their minds. If you experience aphantasia, focus on engaging with other sensory elements you are experiencing around you right now, like taste, touch, and sound. By directing your attention to these sensory experiences, you can create a meaningful sensory soothing practice that aligns with your perception of the world.

# Create a Healthy Sleep Routine
## Sleep

Autistic people face a host of sleep issues, such as difficulties falling asleep, insomnia, reduced REM sleep, sleep apnea, narcolepsy, and more. The reasons behind these challenges are myriad—from genetic mutations affecting melatonin regulation and circadian rhythms (sleep-wake cycles) to sensory sensitivities and busy minds.

If you aren't getting quality sleep, you're more prone to depression, anxiety, executive functioning struggles, and many physical ailments. That's why prioritizing your sleep is a very important part of your self-care program. Two ways to do that are by establishing a healthy sleep routine and setting up a sleep-friendly environment.

A bedtime routine provides consistent cues to your brain and body that it's time to sleep. These reminders are especially important for people who struggle to perceive internal cues of sleepiness. Whether it's due to a flattened melatonin curve, where the natural sleep-wake signals may not be as distinct, or challenges with body awareness, you may not readily recognize when your body is tired. Luckily, you can compensate for this by creating external cues that signal to your mind and body that it's time to sleep.

In addition, you can set up your space to maximize sleep. Your brain constantly looks to create shortcuts; one way it does this is by creating associations. For instance, if you always eat chips while watching your favorite show, your brain starts associating chips with the show. In the same way, if you experience sleep difficulties, your brain may start associating the bedroom with stress and restlessness, perpetuating the insomnia cycle. However, by instead consciously creating *positive* associations with sleep, you can rewire your brain and break free from negative sleep associations.

Here's how to improve your sleep routine and environment:

- **Aim for consistency:** Strive to go to bed at the same time each night. Consistency reinforces the association between the routine and sleep and strengthens your circadian clock.

- **Set the stage for sleep:** Remove distractions and clutter and decorate with what makes you feel cozy and tired, like soft colors and comfortable bedding.

- **Create sleep associations with the bed:** Reserve your bed exclusively for sleep (and sex)—try to avoid using it for work or other activities.

- **Set your bed apart if needed:** For Autistic people, bedrooms often serve as safe spaces to seek refuge. However, frequent retreats to your bedroom can interfere with your brain's associations between the bedroom and sleep. Consider setting up a barrier between your bed and other portions of the room (for example, with a folding room divider or curtain).

- **Create a sleep-friendly environment:** Consider factors such as temperature, lighting, and noise levels.

- **Limit your use of electronic devices for at least an hour before bedtime:** The blue light emitted by screens can interfere with melatonin production and disrupt sleep patterns.

- **Instead, choose calming activities:** Select soothing and relaxing activities that help you unwind and prepare for sleep, such as reading a book, engaging in gentle stretching, or practicing relaxation techniques, such as slow breathing, visualizations, and progressive muscle relaxation.

- **Leverage sensory associations:** Start using sensory cues, such as smelling a particular essential oil or playing soothing music before bed, to signal to your brain that it's time to sleep.

By creating associations like these, you can reshape your brain's neural pathways, minimize insomnia, and promote healthier sleep patterns.

# Put Your Mind to Sleep
## *Sleep*

Autistic people often have busy minds, making it incredibly challenging to fall asleep. You might find yourself consumed by anxious rumination, persistent worry, or a relentless flow of thoughts and ideas. One of the most helpful strategies I've learned for redirecting a busy mind is something called cognitive shuffling.

Cognitive shuffling is the process of intentionally scrambling your thoughts to the point where they no longer follow a logical sequence. It's a technique that can distract and redirect your mind, and it also mimics the cognitive activity typically experienced during the initial stages of sleep. Cognitive shuffling disrupts the evaluative part of your mind and stops it from doing things like planning, problem-solving, and ruminating—thought cycles that tend to keep you awake! By engaging in this exercise, you can break free from the cycle of overthinking and create a mental space that ultimately aids the transition to peaceful slumber.

Some apps, such as MySleepButton, will walk you through a cognitive shuffling exercise.

Try cognitive shuffling independently by following these instructions:

1. Choose a word to begin with, such as "rain," "ocean," or "forest."

2. Start with the first letter of the chosen word; in the case of "rain," you'd start with "r." Think of another word that starts with that letter, like "river." If possible, create a mental image of a flowing river. If you have aphantasia and cannot visualize, simply recall the word without visualization. Now think of another word that begins with the letter "r," such as "rhinoceros" or "rabbit," and bring it to mind. Keep going until you have exhausted all the words starting with "r."

3. Move on to the following letter in the original word, in this case "a." Repeat the process by thinking of words that begin with "a" and visualizing related mental images.

4. Continue this practice, progressing through each letter of the original word, gradually allowing yourself to drift off into sleep. Should any stressful thoughts arise and capture your attention, simply acknowledge them, and gently guide your focus back to the letter you were most recently contemplating.

Give cognitive shuffling a try and see if you can effectively divert your mind's attention, therefore creating a mental state conducive to falling asleep.

# Create a Sensory Sleep Haven
## *Sleep*

Another factor often influencing Autistic sleep is sensory issues! The world around you can easily disrupt your slumber, whether it's unwelcome noises from the neighborhood, the struggle to find comfort, or being particular about temperature and airflow.

You might hesitate to invest in sleep supports that could address some of these issues (like high-quality sheets or an eye mask) because they feel extravagant. But try switching the narrative and thinking of them as helpful accommodations for your sensory needs—and forms of self-care too!

When you take charge of your environment, it can help you feel a sense of empowerment and agency, since you are addressing your own needs. It's not about extravagance; it's about recognizing and taking ownership of your life.

Here are some practical sensory items that can accommodate common sleep issues for Autistic people:

- **Eye mask or blackout curtains:** Drown out intrusive light by enveloping yourself in darkness with a top-notch eye mask or blackout curtains.

- **Sound machine or earplugs:** If you find yourself sensitive to sounds, consider a sound machine or reliable earplugs to block out noise. If earplugs are uncomfortable for you, consider using a Bluetooth sleeping headband.

- **High-quality bedding:** Sleep is a tactile affair, and your bedding plays a crucial role. Seek out pillows and mattresses that cater to your sensory preferences. Explore materials, textures, and weights that soothe you. Note that this may change seasonally; for example, you might prefer a more breathable weighted blanket in summer and a softer and warmer weighted blanket during winter.

- **Fan:** Consider investing in a fan for natural cooling and increased air circulation if you find comfort in gentle breezes.

- **Separate beds or bedrooms:** This topic can spark debate, but it's essential to conduct your own analysis of the potential benefits and drawbacks. Many marriage/partnership guides emphasize the importance of sleeping together, suggesting that sleeping separately may signal trouble. However, my personal experience has shown otherwise. For example, when I am not disturbed by my partner's snoring throughout the night, and when they are not affected by my ADHD bedroom mess and late-night shenanigans, we get along much better. Opting to sleep separately doesn't automatically indicate relationship issues; it can simply mean recognizing that quality sleep leads to increased patience and harmony in the relationship.

Experiment, explore, and fine-tune your sleep haven until it becomes a cherished space befitting your sensory preferences!

# Embrace Adaptive Self-Care Practices
## *Body Care and Hygiene*

As Autistic people, our relationship with our bodies can be complex, and it is often reflected in our approach to self-care. For this reason, we often benefit from building accommodations tailored to our challenges. Let's explore some key factors that can impact our body-related self-care.

- **Body awareness:** Interoception refers to how your body communicates with your mind. Interoception struggles make it difficult to recognize bodily sensations such as thirst, hunger, and the need to use the bathroom.

- **Executive functioning and demands:** Body maintenance is an ongoing process that requires consistent effort. From trimming nails to prepping food, these tasks can present additional stress for people with executive functioning challenges.

While these create additional barriers, they are also things you can accommodate if need be! By building accommodations that address these specific challenges, you can improve your self-care. Here's how:

Interoception Adaptations

- **Create a visual schedule:** Creating visual reminders to provide visual cues for tasks like using the bathroom, drinking water, and eating is a great way to keep them front of mind.

- **Set timers:** Utilize alarms and timers as reminders to check in with yourself, eat regular meals, drink fluids, and use the bathroom. Since your body may not always register thirst and hunger cues, external cues become essential in ensuring proper nutrition and hydration. You can set these up on your phone if you prefer that method.

- **Try setting goals:** Consider setting goals to address interoception challenges. For example, invest in a 32-ounce water bottle and set a goal to empty it by the end of the day. (This goal serves as a concrete reminder to prioritize hydration, which compensates for the fact you may not be receiving internal signals of thirst.)

## Executive Functioning Adaptations

- **Visual reminders and checklists:** Create reminders and checklists for daily self-care tasks. Or use apps like Tiimo to visualize this process.
- **Simplified routines:** Break down self-care routines into smaller, manageable steps. Use visual or written prompts to guide each step of the routine. Simplify choices by organizing food options or health care products in a way that reduces decision-making overload.

You deserve a self-care routine that respects your interoception and executive functioning needs. Embrace accommodations that nurture your well-being!

# Take Care of Personal Hygiene
## *Body Care and Hygiene*

Personal hygiene does not always come easy to Autistic people. Due to heightened sensory sensitivities, daily hygiene practices like bathing, brushing teeth, and grooming can feel overwhelming. When it comes to personal hygiene, it's crucial to approach it with a sensory-friendly lens. Understanding the sensory triggers that make certain tasks uncomfortable allows you to brainstorm adaptations and find alternative solutions.

This simple equation can help you break down the process:

Identify Specific Sensory Triggers

+ Brainstorm Personalized Adaptations

= Effective Self-Care

Begin by identifying the sensory triggers that create discomfort. These triggers can vary from person to person and may include sensitivities to touch, smells, sounds, or other sensory inputs. Once you have identified your sensory triggers, the next step is to brainstorm personalized adaptations. This involves exploring different strategies, products, or modifications that can help reduce your sensory discomfort and make the experience more tolerable.

Here are some examples of swaps and adaptations you can consider to accommodate sensory needs:

- Oral care accommodations: Explore alternative toothbrushes with softer bristles and experiment with different flavors of toothpaste. If toothbrushing is challenging, consider using a silicone chewing tool or a vibrating toothbrush for added sensory input. Consider a toothpaste pump if getting toothpaste on your hands or dyspraxia is an issue.

- **Sensory-friendly bathing:** Create a sensory-friendly bathing experience by using soft or textured towels and using a portable heater to heat the room (to minimize temperature transitions). If having water on your face makes showering challenging, consider using a shower cap to block some water from getting on your face. Dry shampoo can be a convenient alternative to washing your hair with water.

- **Scent sensitivity:** If the smells of deodorant, soaps, and/or shampoos trigger headaches or nausea, explore chemical-free, toxin-free, or unscented alternatives. Various body care options that prioritize sensitivity and offer scent-free or hypoallergenic formulations are available. Many people with scent sensitivities do better once they switch to more natural, chemical-free options.

- **Hand-washing sensory challenges:** If the sensations of traditional soap or hand sanitizers are bothersome, experiment with different textures and consistencies. Foaming soaps may offer a more tolerable experience. Additionally, exploring alternatives such as hand-sanitizing wipes or gels with soothing ingredients can provide a sensory-friendly option.

- **Skin-care sensitivities:** Many Autistic people get rashes with popular lotions and skin-care products. Explore gentle and fragrance-free options specifically designed for sensitive skin. Look for products with minimal ingredients and consider patch testing new products on a small area of skin before incorporating them into your routine.

These examples are starting points—everyone's sensory experiences and preferences vary, so do what feels right to you. You deserve a hygiene routine that honors your sensory needs!

# Tune Into Your Body's Signals with a Body Scan

## Body Care and Hygiene

One way to care for your physical self is by strengthening your connection to your body (this is also known as interoception awareness). Even if you currently struggle with interoception, it is like a muscle in that the more you practice using it, the stronger you'll get! When you improve your body awareness, you are better able to manage your body's needs and respond to your emotions.

One exercise that promotes increased body awareness is the body scan.

Here's how to conduct a body scan:

1. Find a comfortable space where you can focus without distractions.

2. Begin by focusing on your toes and assessing how they feel. Avoid judging or evaluating these sensations; instead, use neutral descriptions like "tingling," "tight," or "relaxed."

3. Gradually scan upward to your head, paying attention to any sensations in each body part.

4. As you progress with body scan practice, you can begin linking bodily sensations to your emotions. For example, when you feel angry, you might notice that your shoulders are tense.

Remember, you are looking to notice and identify bodily signals without attaching meaning to them. The goal of the body scan is not to judge or change the sensations you are experiencing, but simply to cultivate a non-judgmental and curious attitude toward your body.

If sensations are difficult for you to describe, try using other descriptors like color (e.g., "it feels purple"). You may discover your own unique language for expressing bodily sensations, so don't hesitate to get creative and find the language that resonates with you!

# Integrate Body Awareness Into Daily Activities

## Body Care and Hygiene

While you can build body awareness through direct activities, like body scans, some people might find them too intrusive or challenging (especially if you have a history of trauma). Or, for others, adding another exercise to your daily routine might not sound feasible. If you fall into those categories, you can instead incorporate interoception builders into your daily routines.

Interoception exercises can be boiled down to this simple equation:

### Create a Sensation + Notice It

The first step is to create a sensation—you can do this by creating tension, such as squeezing your muscles or pressing your hands together. Alternatively, you can generate a sensation by touching something soft, cool, hot, or bumpy. The second step, "notice," simply involves directing your attention to the sensation, ideally without judgment or evaluation.

Here are two ways to incorporate interoception into your routine:

1. Integrate interoceptive builders into activities: Think about your daily rituals and identify ones where you could reflect for a moment while you do them. For example, as you drink your morning tea or coffee, take a moment to feel the warmth of the cup in your hands.

2. Set alarms as reminders: Set two alarms throughout the day. When each alarm goes off, do a thirty-second interoception check-in. Focus your attention on a specific bodily sensation, such as the feeling of your feet on the ground or the rhythm of your breath.

By incorporating these activities into your day, you can build interoception awareness without adding an overwhelming task to your to-do list!

# Manage Food Challenges:
# Executive Function and Sensory Tips
## *Body Care and Hygiene*

Nutrition is a complex topic for Autistic people, as it involves navigating numerous obstacles. These challenges may range from sensory challenges to executive functioning difficulties to gastrointestinal issues and co-occurring conditions like Avoidant/Restrictive Food Intake Disorder (ARFID). In this entry, we'll focus on executive functioning and sensory barriers tips.

### Executive Functioning Accommodations

Common executive functioning challenges in this area include challenges with planning, organization, and time management. We might have trouble laying out the steps for making a meal, getting all the ingredients and tools organized, guessing how long each task will take, and juggling multiple tasks at once. Here are some accommodations to consider:

- **Stock up on preprepared or frozen meals:** Keep a supply of preprepared or frozen meals on hand for those low-energy days when you don't feel like cooking.

- **Explore meal-subscription services:** If budget allows, explore meal-subscription services or subscription boxes for convenient, preprepared meals and ingredients, reducing executive functioning demands.

- **Break down meal planning:** Simplify meal planning by dividing it into steps: select recipes, create a shopping list, and set a cooking schedule. Visual planners or meal-planning apps can help streamline the process further.

- **Create a routine:** Establishing a consistent meal routine such as "Taco Tuesdays" can reduce decision fatigue.

- **Utilize visual supports for recipes:** When cooking, look for recipes with step-by-step pictorial instructions. Visual instructions tend to work well for Autistic brains because they provide a clear visual road map of each cooking step.

## Sensory Accommodations

Sensory barriers can also get in the way of meal prep and eating. Here are a few sensory tips to consider:

- **Safe Foods:** First off, it's good to know what your "safe foods" are—those go-to foods you can eat even when sensory overload hits. Make sure you keep them stocked up!

- **Sensory Environment:** Eating can be quite a sensory experience. So, when you're trying new foods or working on broadening your nutritional horizons, choose a low-anxiety, sensory-friendly environment. A bustling family meal or a noisy cafeteria are not the best places to test your sensory boundaries!

- **Nutrient-Dense Formats:** Do some experimentation and try to find nutrient-dense formats that you enjoy (or can tolerate). For example, smoothies are a structure I can tolerate, so I work hard to pack my nutrition there. One of my kids loves smoothie bowls with crunchy toppings like granola and coconut. Others might lean into nutrient-dense baked goods like muffins. Once you've found a format that clicks with you, focus on expanding your nutrition there, all while keeping your trusty, safe foods on standby when you need them. Having one nutrient-dense source you can tolerate can ease the pressure elsewhere, allowing you to revert to your safe foods as needed while ensuring your body is getting some of those key nutrients it deserves!

Using tips like these to identify your particular executive functioning or sensory barriers and build accommodations around them can reduce stress while nurturing your body.

# Supplement with Vitamins
## *Body Care and Hygiene*

Due to sensory sensitivities and food allergies, many Autistic people have narrow diets. There is no problem with seeking comfort through predictable foods and meals. However, it can create some challenges for your gut health and overall nutrient consumption. In fact, research indicates that Autistic people often experience deficiencies in certain minerals and nutrients. Addressing these nutritional gaps is another way to support your physical self-care.

While you should talk to your medical providers, because individual needs vary, here are some nutrients that research suggests may be lower in Autistic people:

- **Vitamin D:** Essential for mood regulation, bone health, immune function, muscle strength, cognitive health, and heart health, vitamin D may also play a role in cancer prevention.

- **Omega-3 fatty acids:** These essential fatty acids are crucial for brain health and function.

- **Magnesium:** Magnesium is involved in various bodily functions, including muscle relaxation, nerve function, and sleep regulation.

- **Zinc:** Zinc is essential to immune function, cognition, and sensory regulation.

- **B vitamins:** Several B vitamins, such as folate (vitamin $B_9$) and vitamin $B_{12}$, may be lower (or we may have more difficulty absorbing). These vitamins are essential for energy production and neurological function.

You can help ensure your body receives these and other essential nutrients by seeking out nutrient-dense foods and/or supplementing your dietary intake with high-quality vitamins. Again, work with your medical providers—a primary care provider, nutritionist, and/or naturopath—to figure out a personalized plan you can follow.

# CHAPTER THREE

• • •

# Emotional Self-Care

The world that Autistic people inhabit does not align with our neurological and communication styles. This, plus our heightened nervous system, makes us particularly vulnerable to emotional struggles. For this reason, it is especially important that you prioritize your emotional self-care. Emotional self-care is anything you do that helps develop emotional awareness and strengthen your resilience. In this chapter, you'll explore activities in several categories that will help you cultivate emotional self-care:

- **Managing Autistic burnout:** By reducing emotional demands, recognizing early signs of burnout, and clearing your mind, you can regain a sense of control and address your emotions with greater empowerment.

- **Setting boundaries and self-advocacy:** You can help protect your emotional well-being by setting boundaries, unmasking, and advocating for yourself.

- **Cultivating emotional awareness, literacy, and resilience:** Simply having the words to describe your feelings is a powerful skill that can help you identify and process your emotions.

- **Regulating emotions:** Think of emotion regulation skills as your toolbox for managing those intense feelings so you can work through them effectively. Techniques like labeling your emotions and grounding yourself can help fine-tune your emotion regulation skills.

By leaning into Autistic strengths, such as an exceptional eye for detail and pattern recognition, you can approach your emotions with curiosity and care.

# Prioritize Rest to Avoid Burnout
## *Autistic Burnout*

Did you know that burnout is one of the causes of depression and suicidality for Autistic people? Do you know what one of the causes of burnout is? Not getting sufficient rest!

Autistic people need a lot of rest. Indeed, the sheer amount needed can be frustrating. Yet the alternative—a debilitating burnout—is even less appealing. So one of the best things you can do for your emotional health is to prioritize rest.

Prioritizing rest can be difficult for many people, especially those driven by an internal belief that you should be able to just "push through"—a notion often tied to internalized ableism. A propensity to people-please as a coping mechanism for social differences might also hamper your ability to rest. In these cases, overcoming your internalized ableism is crucial in unlocking your capacity for rest.

Additionally, your notion of rest may differ from allistic norms. For instance, conventional self-care rituals like spa days, often relished by allistic individuals, may sound terrible to you. These types of activities are quite stressful to me—I instead find solace and restoration in engaging with my interests, learning, and creative pursuits.

Your version of rest might entail reading a favorite book, listening to your favorite podcast, or hiking in nature—a form of "restorative rest." Avoid falling into the trap of "cheap rest"—those quick fixes like binge-watching TV shows—which may provide fleeting gratification yet leave you feeling more drained.

The crucial aspect is not how your rest aligns with societal norms but whether it rejuvenates and restores you. Embrace your distinct forms of rest and allow them to revitalize you.

# Engage In Sensory Detox
## *Autistic Burnout*

When I worked in hospitals and universities, I would invariably return home each night shrouded in palpable fatigue and plagued by a persistent, low-grade fever. It was a puzzling malaise that seemed to persist without a discernible cause. My revelation came when I realized I was experiencing sensory overload to such a degree that my body was interpreting it as a physical illness. My Autistic child and I now refer to these as "sensory sick" moments, when we feel the wear and tear of a high-sensory day.

Once the onset of "sensory sickness" begins to creep in, I know it's time to initiate my sensory-detox routine—a series of calming and restorative activities designed to rebalance my sensory system. This might involve taking a hot shower to cleanse and refresh, changing into my most comfortable clothes, or sinking into a bean bag chair cloaked in a weighted blanket while indulging in the rhythm of my favorite stim song. I might also turn to my trusty TENS unit for relief. (TENS units, short for Transcutaneous Electrical Nerve Stimulation units, are these handy devices that provide mini electrical zaps or pulses. While they are predominantly used for pain, they also work to provide repetitive sensory input.) When I engage in these rituals, I can feel the harsh sensory residue of the day gradually dissolve.

Your sensory detox will be as unique as your sensory profile. While I find solace in stillness and weighted comfort, you might prefer an energetic walk or music. Explore and identify what suits you, then curate your sensory-detox ritual—a haven for those intense high-sensory days when "sensory sickness" looms.

# Identify Signs of Autistic Burnout
## *Autistic Burnout*

Many Autistic people face Autistic burnout, which is often brought about by striving to meet allistic expectations, demands, and pace of life without suitable support structures. Autistic burnout manifests as profound fatigue, heightened sensory sensitivities, and a loss of skills, particularly executive functioning and speech abilities. Although distinct from depression, it often culminates in depression if left unchecked.

Identifying the signs of Autistic burnout is essential for gauging your boundaries, implementing self-care measures, and reaching out for support when necessary.

Let's explore some key signs you should be watchful for:

- **Unrelenting fatigue:** Persistent exhaustion, even after adequate rest and sleep, is a key part of Autistic burnout. When grappling with burnout, your body may feel utterly exhausted, leaving you scrambling for energy to complete even the simplest tasks.

- **Heightened sensory sensitivities:** Sensitivity to sensory stimuli—be it noise, light, texture, or smell—intensifies during burnout, amplifying your susceptibility to sensory overload, meltdowns, and shutdowns. Sensory stimuli that used to feel manageable may now feel overwhelming.

- **Skills and functioning decline:** A conspicuous drop in skills like focusing, organizing, problem-solving, and speaking is another feature of burnout and makes social interactions more daunting.

- **Emotional dysregulation:** Burnout-induced dysregulation in your nervous and sensory systems hampers your ability to manage your emotions, resulting in intense emotions or emotional numbness. Increased anxiety, irritability, or feelings of being overwhelmed are common during burnout.

- **Diminished tolerance for change:** During burnout, your capacity to absorb and adapt to change wanes, and you may seek comfort in sameness and predictability. You might experience heightened distress in the face of the unexpected.

- **Social isolation:** Burnout can spark a retreat into solitude and diminish your ability to engage socially. You might withdraw from social interactions and lose motivation for once-enjoyed hobbies or activities.

- **Masking:** Burnout can throw a wrench in your masking abilities, and it can be confusing if you don't understand what is happening! Interestingly, lots of adults don't get their autism diagnosis until they are in burnout and have lost their ability to mask.

Being in tune with these early signs of Autistic burnout is vital for your proactive engagement in emotional self-care. Once you start noticing these signals, you understand it's time to use your SOS self-care tools and/or ask for the support you need. Try to alleviate some of your burdens where possible by dropping demands, establishing healthy boundaries, and engaging in sensory detox (use other entries in this book for ideas).

This proactive approach doesn't just help manage burnout—it helps prevent a potential downward spiral into depression. Aim to view these signs not as threats but as gentle reminders from your body and mind to pause and take care of yourself.

# Drop Unnecessary Demands
## Autistic Burnout

As explored in the Identify Signs of Autistic Burnout entry earlier in this chapter, Autistic people are prone to burnout. Complicating matters, we tend to blur the lines between essential and nonessential demands, a manifestation of our all-or-nothing thinking pattern and inclination toward perfectionism. Many of us tend to pile on extra pressure and demands, and that often leads to burnout, cognitive overload, feelings of being overwhelmed, stress, and anxiety! It can turn into this never-ending cycle that takes us on an emotional roller coaster.

It's especially important to consider what demands to drop when you're in burnout. However, your mind likely gets cloudy during burnout, making this distinction even more challenging. Therefore, it's beneficial to prepare ahead of time by earmarking which demands can be let go. Having a ready-to-go list of "droppable" demands can be a lifesaver on high-sensory days or when burnout signs start to surface.

Consider employing a traffic light system for your responsibilities, categorizing demands into green, yellow, and red activities. Green tasks can be put aside without notable ramifications. Yellow tasks can occasionally be set aside, depending on prevailing circumstances. Red tasks pose more of a challenge to dismiss, given the potentially significant repercussions.

In our home, for instance, family dinner is a "green light" demand—one that can be sidelined on a high-sensory day. Even routine activities like showering can be deferred (though perhaps not for a five-day stretch!).

By proactively pinpointing droppable demands, you can more effectively navigate burnout periods. You'll have already made decisions on what to let go, thus allowing you to eliminate further decision fatigue and prioritize rest.

# Find Solace in Familiar Stories

## *Autistic Burnout*

For Autistic people, there's a unique comfort found in the familiar rhythms of repetition and predictability. That's why revisiting your cherished movies or rereading your favorite books can offer you profound comfort and solace when you encounter feelings of being overwhelmed, stress, or anxiety.

After journeying through the unpredictable terrain of an allistic world, the known world of your much-loved narratives provides a comforting haven. Knowing the course of the story, with its highs and lows, imparts a calming certainty to your mind.

And let's be honest—there's just something magical about revisiting a beloved story that you know inside and out. Each encounter uncovers previously overlooked nuances, or it rekindles your initial affection for the tale. It's akin to spending time with a longtime, trusted companion.

Burnout or overstimulation, however, can cloud your decision-making abilities and even obscure your memory so you have a hard time remembering your favorites. To counteract this, make a list of your top choices ahead of time so you can refer to them easily whenever you need them.

You can create a playlist of beloved songs, jot down on your phone a list of your go-to TV shows, or assign a specific place in your home for your favorite books so they're easy to spot when you need them. Dedicate some time to compile a reservoir of your cherished pieces, making them readily accessible. This simple idea may not seem momentous, but when you need support ASAP, having your lists already made or your items in an easy-to-find spot will help you soothe yourself that much faster.

# Clear Emotional Clutter
# with a Brain Dump
## *Autistic Burnout*

Neurodivergent minds house an intricate web of connections, associations, and ceaseless activity. This continuous buzz can complicate decision-making and task completion, impede restful sleep, and cause stress and anxiety.

To help process those difficult feelings, consider doing a "brain dump." Think of a brain dump as a mental cleanse where you transcribe the whirlwind of thoughts and emotions in your head onto paper. This act of transcription releases the brain from its perceived obligation to remember, allowing your mind to feel free and clear.

One of the chief benefits of a brain dump lies in its potential to alleviate any stress and anxiety you may feel. The swirling chaos of ideas and thoughts can impede focus, but by transferring this chaos onto paper, you unburden your mind, clear your mental pathways, and reduce stress. Additionally, a brain dump allows you to reclaim valuable mental real estate. This newfound clarity and spaciousness can stimulate creativity, enhance focus, and promote a more profound sense of peace and satisfaction. In essence, a brain dump not only clears your mind but also curates an internal environment primed for other types of self-care, like rest, innovation, and self-reflection.

There are many ways to try a brain dump. You can try them all and see which one works best for you, or just jump to the one that resonates most strongly with you.

Here are several ways to try brain dumping:

- **Task dump:** Write down your to-do list to tidy your mind and prioritize tasks.
- **Free-association dump:** Write down *all* the thoughts in your mind, even if they are not connected to one another.
- **Idea dump:** Note all your creative sparks, big and small.
- **Organization dump:** Draft a mind map or concept map to systematically arrange your thoughts for a task or project. (See the Map Out Your Thoughts entry in this chapter for instructions.)
- **Stress dump:** List all the things stressing you out. This will help declutter your mind and clear mental fog.
- **Gratitude dump:** Write down everything you're grateful for. This process shifts your focus from negative thoughts to more positive aspects of life.
- **Emotional dump:** Without judgment or analysis, note all the emotions you're experiencing. This exercise can help you gain clarity about your emotional state and identify and release suppressed feelings.
- **Nighttime dump:** If a bustling mind is making it hard for you to sleep, consider writing down whatever is in your brain before bedtime.

In addition to stress and anxiety relief, brain dumps can be beneficial for people grappling with executive functioning challenges, particularly for "AuDHDers" (Autistic people with ADHD). Brain dumps can help AuDHDers with organizing and visualizing thoughts, prioritizing tasks, and deconstructing projects into manageable steps.

Undertaking a brain dump using whatever method works for you can be a powerful self-care strategy to manage stress, cleanse your mind, and restore your equilibrium.

# Part Ways with Masking
## Boundaries and Self-Advocacy

Have you ever noticed yourself instinctively adopting someone else's accent, body language, or behavior during a conversation? This phenomenon, often experienced among Autistic people who mask, transforms us into conversational chameleons.

Many Autistic people, driven by an innate drive for safety, adapt to social differences by masking. We become adept at sensing others' needs and adjusting ourselves to meet them. This ability can become so deeply ingrained that it permeates your language and mannerisms. While it's a clever survival strategy, it has significant drawbacks. Autistic masking is often linked with heightened anxiety and depression levels. Furthermore, when you consistently mold your identity based on others' needs, it becomes challenging to establish your sense of self.

Again, masking is rooted in an innate need for safety. Many BIPOC Autistic people are navigating the double layer of masking and code-switching. To safely unmask, you must first feel safe, therefore the conversation of unmasking must always be held within the same conversation as safety, especially for the most marginalized within the Autistic community.

Even when you're in a safe environment, unlearning masking behaviors can be a challenging process that involves several things, such as:

- **Acknowledging** and confronting Autistic shame
- **Establishing** healthy boundaries
- **Prioritizing** your own needs and desires

But before you can effectively communicate and set boundaries, you need to start at a more fundamental level—by discovering your preferences! The first step toward shedding the chameleon skin is to invest time in discovering your own desires, wants, and needs.

Here's a good way to start: Conduct self-check-ins once or twice a day, solely to connect with your current wants and needs. Ask yourself, "What do I need right now?" or "What do I want right now?" For instance, during a conversation, instead of wondering whether the other person is enjoying the conversation or if you're causing any embarrassment, flip the narrative and instead ask yourself, "Am I enjoying this conversation? Do *I* want to continue this conversation?"

The first step toward breaking free from masking is learning to tune into yourself. If you've spent a lifetime tapping into the needs of others, you likely struggle to tune into your own inner world.

Once you have clarity on your needs and wants, you can begin to set boundaries and communicate assertively (see the Discover the Power of Self-Advocacy in this chapter for more on this topic).

Be mindful to extend kindness and compassion toward yourself throughout this journey of unmasking. It's natural to feel uncertain or uncomfortable as you explore your true self and unlearn habitual masking behaviors. Recognize that this process is not about forcing change but rather about gently allowing authenticity to surface at its own pace. Celebrate the small victories, and don't get disheartened by the setbacks. Remember that you're not alone; many Autistic people are walking this path alongside you. Sharing your experiences with supportive communities can provide a sense of camaraderie and shared understanding. Most importantly, remember that every step you take toward authenticity is a testament to your strength and resilience.

# Discover the Power of Self-Advocacy
## *Boundaries and Self-Advocacy*

The concept of self-advocacy may initially seem daunting to you—but it can be as straightforward as requesting a different seat or seeking clarification on a puzzling question. In essence, self-advocacy involves voicing your needs. As an Autistic individual, it often falls on you to request the accommodations that enable you to function optimally in a world typically tailored to the needs of allistic bodies and minds.

The process of self-advocacy can be streamlined by keeping the following equation in mind:

$$\text{Self-Disclosure} + \text{Request} = \text{Self-Advocacy}$$

Self-advocacy frequently involves intertwining a disclosure about a particular need with a specific request. While the disclosure part isn't always necessary, it's this pairing that morphs it into a powerful act of self-advocacy.

For instance, I recently found myself seated at a restaurant at a metallic table under glaring artificial light. The metallic odor proved overwhelming. I asked the server if I could relocate, explaining, "I have sensory sensitivities, and the metallic aroma is making me nauseated. Could I possibly switch to a wooden table?" The server graciously complied, and I found myself in a comfortable spot with natural lighting and a wooden table.

Let's look at a few more examples of the self-advocacy equation in action:

- "I have auditory-processing differences, which makes it hard for me to hear in loud environments. Can we continue our conversation outside?"

- "I thrive on direct communication. Would you mind elaborating on your feedback so I can better understand how to improve?"

It's crucial to remember that full disclosure is not a prerequisite for self-advocacy. Partial self-disclosure, such as mentioning "sensory differences," "auditory-processing difficulty," or "a preference for direct communication," is completely acceptable. Or you can simply request what you need without any explanation at all. Articulating your specific needs and making a request is particularly assertive and effective self-advocacy.

Sometimes jotting down a quick script ahead of time can make the interaction go more smoothly. To practice, reflect on the past week, identifying situations where accommodations would have been beneficial. Using the self-advocacy equation, create scripts for those scenarios. Or consider common experiences you have and write self-advocacy scripts for those. Practice reciting these scripts aloud. Keep your comfort level with self-disclosure in mind and modify the scripts as needed.

Self-advocacy is a powerful skill, and like any skill, it can be honed with practice. Don't berate yourself if you stumble in your initial attempts. In addition, there will unfortunately be instances where you might face resistance or misunderstanding. Such reactions often stem from a lack of knowledge about neurodivergence and are not a reflection of your worth or your request's validity. When faced with such responses, reaffirm your worth and remind yourself that you deserve accommodations that allow you to interact with the world. It might be helpful to have a supportive friend or a mentor with whom you can debrief and strategize for future instances. With time, you'll notice that self-advocacy becomes more natural and the hurdles less daunting.

# Dismantle Stereotypes about Autism
## Boundaries and Self-Advocacy

Promoting your rights and asserting your needs can often be challenging due to the widespread misinformation and stereotypes associated with autism. Disclosing your autism can sometimes invite skepticism, invalidation, and questioning—plus, it also often involves providing others with a comprehensive education on autism, which adds to your emotional load.

Let's tackle some common stereotypes and misconceptions. You can use these insights in your daily conversations to dispel myths and advocate for yourself:

- **Empathy:** While some Autistic people have lower levels of empathy, studies have found that this is often related to a condition called alexithymia (a condition causing difficulty in recognizing and naming emotions). Being Autistic doesn't mean we lack empathy. Quite the contrary, many of us experience heightened empathy and possess a deep capacity for understanding and sharing emotions.

- **Rudeness:** Characterized by honesty, authenticity, and directness, Autistic communication may be perceived as rude by some allistic people. However, this perception is a cultural interpretation. Indeed, it could be argued that direct feedback is more respectful than passive-aggressive options.

- **Eye contact:** There is an assumption that Autistic people "can't" make eye contact. Many Autistic people do find sustained eye contact uncomfortable. Neuroimaging studies have shown heightened amygdala activation during such interactions, indicating that our fear center becomes more activated, making sustained eye contact a more stressful and emotionally charged experience but is not a physical impossibility.

- **Conversational skills:** Engaging in reciprocal conversation, especially small talk, can be challenging for many Autistic people. However, this discomfort tends to lessen when discussing areas of interest or when interacting with other Autistic people. Thus, context and topic are significant contributors to our conversational capabilities.

- **Relationships and sexuality:** Autistic people encompass a diverse spectrum of sexual and romantic inclinations. Many of us form long-term partnerships, have children, and build families, underscoring the diversity and richness of our experiences.

- **Aggression:** Harming others is not a common trait associated with autism—in fact, the majority of us are much more likely to harm ourselves than harm others. Instances of aggression, such as mass shootings, typically involve coexisting conditions or external influences. Meltdowns, which may result in aggression, often occur when communication attempts through other means have been dismissed. It is crucial to recognize the root causes and triggers of such behaviors.

- **Emotional experience:** Alexithymia, if present, can make identifying and expressing emotions challenging for some Autistic people. However, many of us harbor intricate and profoundly emotional inner lives. Our unique ways of expressing and experiencing emotions may differ from neuronormative standards, but our emotional experiences are deep and impactful.

- **Intelligence:** Autistic people span the full intellectual spectrum, similar to allistic individuals. The stereotype of unintelligence is often fueled by the prevalence of coexisting intellectual disabilities among diagnosed Autistic people. On the other hand, media portrayals of Autistic people as geniuses or savants have perpetuated the misconception that we're all extraordinarily intelligent. In truth, we exhibit a broad range of intellectual capabilities.

By dismantling autism stereotypes, you can help lay the groundwork for a world that acknowledges the diverse experiences of Autistic people.

# Manage Hyper-Empathy
## *Boundaries and Self-Advocacy*

Similar to how an Autistic person may be hyper- or hyposensitive to sensory experiences, an Autistic person can also be hypo-empathetic (have difficulty accessing emotions of empathy) or hyper-empathetic (have heightened sensitivity to the pain of others).

Hyper-empathetic people are deeply impacted by the energy and emotions of those around them. Additionally, they are hypersensitive to the suffering in the world. They absorb and are profoundly affected by the emotional atmosphere. This is also my experience, and I've often used the metaphor that it is like I have porous skin—it's full of holes that allow everything to enter. My skin often fails to shield me from the world. It fails to keep out the constant influx. Those of us who live with "porous skin" are chronically bombarded with the emotions and energy of the people around us.

To compensate, I craft "artificial skin." My routines, special interests, repetitions, rituals, boundaries, and deliberate decisions create a carefully constructed barrier. This artificial skin provides an added layer of protection. If you, too, absorb the emotions around you, consider the following ways to create your artificial skin and shield your porous self:

- **Implement routines and rituals:** Establish consistent routines and engage in rituals that bring you comfort and stability. These can provide a sense of grounding and help you regulate the overwhelming emotional input.

- **Engage your interests:** Delve into your interests as a form of refuge. Immersing yourself in activities or topics that captivate your attention can create a shield against the emotional intensity of others and help your mind unhook from the suffering of the world.

- **Choose your company wisely:** Spend time with people whose energy positively influences you, as their emotions can significantly impact you.

- **Establish healthy boundaries:** Set and maintain boundaries to safeguard your emotional well-being. Prioritize your needs and limit emotional demands.

- **Manage your news consumption:** Be mindful of the news you expose yourself to and consider adding filters to protect your nervous system. Painful news stories can easily hijack your nervous system, and the combination of hyper-empathy and hyperfixation can make news cycles particularly painful for Autistic people. Be thoughtful and deliberate in managing your news and social media consumption.

- **Have rituals of releasing:** Whether it's drawing upon mindfulness practices or spiritual practices, find ways to release the weight of the world's pain. For example, at the end of the day, visualize releasing the pain you have taken in throughout the day to a higher power, spirit, the collective unconscious, or just into the air.

- **Embrace agency:** The mix of hyper-empathy and disempowerment can be challenging. Redirect your energy to areas where you can effect positive change. Whether your passion is antiracist efforts, supporting LGBTQIA+ rights, or environmental action, channel your empathy into meaningful action.

By consciously crafting this "artificial skin," you can protect yourself from the negative effects of energy absorption. Instead, use your natural empathy to create good in the world!

# Curtail the Apology Reflex
## Boundaries and Self-Advocacy

Do you habitually apologize, even when others bump into you or when you're simply asking for clarification? Does this apology reflex manifest everywhere in your life? Many Autistic people tend to apologize excessively. It's as if we feel compelled to apologize for our mere existence.

Before realizing I was Autistic and consciously addressing this issue, I found myself apologizing relentlessly. I felt a constant need to justify my existence by being excessively accommodating. Whenever my presence seemed to cause any inconvenience, regardless of fault, an apology would follow. Due to our efforts to fit into a neurotypical society and the shame we experience when we're unable to do so, many of us have become accustomed to apologizing for simply taking up space.

While expressing regret when you genuinely hurt someone or err is important, continually apologizing for merely existing needs reassessment. This reflex reinforces a negative self-narrative of being a burden or an inconvenience, leading to feelings of neurodivergent shame and low self-esteem and adversely affecting our emotional health.

To break free from the apology reflex, try a new response. Next time someone inadvertently bumps into you (or the reverse), use phrases like "Excuse me" or "Pardon me" rather than automatically saying, "I'm sorry." Adjusting your language helps you shift away from constant self-deprecation and fosters a more affirming sense of self. Over time, you can learn to stop apologizing for everything and begin to cultivate a more positive and confident self-image!

# Break Free from Toxic Attachments
## Boundaries and Self-Advocacy

Given that many Autistic people are inherently trusting, coupled with a tendency to people-please, we can be particularly vulnerable to social manipulation. This, paired with difficulty deciphering hidden intentions and manipulative behaviors, further heightens the risk of encountering a toxic relationship.

Toxic relationships are characterized by inconsistent affection and a roller coaster of emotional highs and lows, and they are harmful to a person's psyche. This confusing cycle, even if painful at times, can feel addictive and tough to escape. Recognizing these patterns and their toll on your emotional health is key. When evaluating a relationship, focus on how it makes you feel.

Reflect on the following:

- Are there recurring instances of criticism, manipulation, or control?
- Does it leave you feeling unsafe, anxious, or doubting your self-worth?
- Do I feel comfortable and safe with this person?
- Do they openly criticize or ridicule me?
- Do I feel manipulated by them?
- Do they use affection as a control tactic?
- Do they try to control me?

Choosing to distance yourself from a toxic relationship is hard, but you *can* do it. First, be sure you are physically safe. Then, begin to limit your interactions with the individual. Consider garnering support from trustworthy friends and family or a professional counselor. Cultivating a supportive network can boost confidence and promote emotional balance during this transition.

Drawing lines and breaking free from toxic ties are not only bold acts of self-protection—they're powerful assertions of your intrinsic value.

# Map Out Your Thoughts
## Emotional Awareness, Literacy, and Resilience

Mapping out your thoughts can be a powerful way to increase emotional self-awareness and organize your thinking. Thought mapping goes beyond a simple brain dump (as discussed in the Clear Emotional Clutter with a Brain Dump entry in this chapter). This technique is about making visible the connections, ties, and patterns among your thoughts.

The Autistic brain naturally thinks in associations and patterns, which is why answering questions can sometimes feel like a marathon! Our brains want to provide *all* the context and describe *all* the associations. We often perceive the interconnections and patterns, creating a sophisticated and intricate web inside our minds, much like a Wikipedia page, as poignantly described by Autistic comedian Hannah Gadsby.

Traditional problem-solving methods like pros-and-cons lists or compartmentalized strategies may not suit your brain's associative style. Thought mapping, a method that allows you to visualize connections between ideas, can be a great alternative. Thought mapping allows you to illustrate the relationships between ideas, feelings, and issues, a boon for emotional awareness.

Whether you're brainstorming for a project, solving a problem, or chalking out a life plan, here's how you get started:

1. Start by jotting down your central theme or problem in the center of a page. Circle it for emphasis.

2. Next, identify subthemes or factors that contribute to the main theme or problem. If your central issue is stress, for example, potential subcategories could include stress from school, relationships, or work.

3. Connect each subcategory to the central circle with lines, creating a web of related topics.

4. Go deeper by adding more bubbles to each subcategory. For example, under "school stress," you might **pinpoint** issues like a difficult research paper.

5. Continue **expanding** your map, branching out and forming associations as you go.

6. **Reflect** on your completed thought map. Take the time to observe the interconnected issues and patterns that have emerged. This is a chance to gain insights, discover new perspectives, and find potential solutions. Note any revelations or ideas that spring up during this reflective process. This step is key to enhancing emotional awareness and understanding your thought patterns.

Thought maps aren't only for problem-solving; they're also great for highlighting positives, like your values, identities, and things you're thankful for. The beauty of a thought map is its flexibility—you can put anything in the center!

Choosing a thought map over a linear list can be a game changer for associative thinkers and visually inclined minds. Translating your thoughts onto paper not only helps increase emotional awareness; it also eases stress by externalizing thoughts from your mind.

# Grasp Difficult Emotions
## Emotional Awareness, Literacy, and Resilience

When I was in my first year of training to become a psychologist, one of the skills we learned was identifying and labeling other people's emotions. I observed classmates smoothly mastering these emotional-reflection exercises while I stared down at a long list of emotion words struggling to know what to do with them! I couldn't help but wonder why these exercises felt so difficult for me.

It wasn't until I discovered that I was Autistic that my complex relationship with emotions started to make sense. I've always understood my internal landscape through concepts, ideas, analysis, and images. In contrast, the realm of emotions felt like an alien landscape. About half of Autistic folks grapple with alexithymia, a condition causing difficulty in recognizing and naming emotions.

If you can't pin down what you're feeling, boosting your emotional awareness and resilience becomes a tall order. This emotional opacity can hamper your ability to regulate emotions, understand your needs and wants, connect emotionally with others, and even connect to yourself. That's why fostering emotional awareness and literacy is essential.

Here are some practices to help you amplify emotional awareness and literacy when emotions feel elusive:

- **Visualize:** Autistic brains often lean heavily on visual processing. Look online for tools, like an emotion matrix, feeling wheel, or feeling list, which can help convert abstract emotions into concrete visual concepts. You can download several of these for free at NeurodivergentInsights.com.

- **Read:** Fiction can offer valuable insights into emotions. Authors give us windows into characters' emotional landscapes, decoding emotions, intentions, and motivations—thus enhancing emotional understanding.

- **Engage with music or photo prompts:** Stimuli, like music and photos, can spark strong emotional responses. Use these prompts to practice diving deeper into your emotions and enhancing your emotional awareness.

- **Journal for emotional awareness:** Journaling provides an avenue for accessing your inner world in ways that spoken language often cannot. By journaling to identify and explore your emotions, you can increase your awareness of them. Additionally, you can find patterns and identify common themes, triggers, and more.

The world of emotions may seem confusing and disorienting, but with practice, intentionality, and persistence, you will find it easier to navigate. However, cultivating emotional awareness is not an overnight task—it's a journey. Some days it might feel like you're making huge strides, while others it might seem like you're back at square one. That's okay. Patience and persistence are your allies in this process. Over time, you'll notice patterns, gain insights, and understand yourself on a deeper level. Celebrate each small victory along the way—every moment of awareness is a step forward on this journey of emotional literacy. Developing emotional awareness and literacy not only unlocks profound self-discovery but also ushers in a richer understanding of the world.

# Practice Gratitude
## Emotional Awareness, Literacy, and Resilience

I've always been sensitive to experiences where it feels as if someone is trying to manipulate an emotional response out of me, such as with motivational speakers. This is why I used to be a bit skeptical of things like gratitude practices, as they seemed like a form of self-manipulation. However, my perspective changed when I learned the neuroscience behind them and realized that my skepticism wasn't justified. Gratitude practices are not about manipulating yourself to feel something that isn't real. Instead, they prime your brain to be on the lookout for the things in your life that really do bring you joy, connection, meaning, and gratitude. They help balance out your brain and correct for confirmation bias.

Your brain is naturally wired to seek out certain aspects of your environment. So, for example, if you're depressed, your mind tends to focus on negative thoughts about yourself, the world, and the future. Your brain is essentially filtering out anything that would go against your depression and laser focusing on the negative.

Many Autistic people are predisposed to view life through a more anxious or depressed lens, and cultivating gratitude can counteract that confirmation bias. By incorporating gratitude into your life, you provide a counterbalance, allowing you to shift your focus and actively seek out moments of goodness amid the challenges of life. Rather than blocking out the reality of your experience, gratitude practices offer a broader perspective and help you appreciate the positive aspects that may be easily overlooked.

Starting a gratitude practice doesn't have to be a taxing endeavor.

Here are three simple ways to incorporate gratitude into your life:

1. **Think of three good things:** At the end of each day, list three good things that happened. They could be as simple as a beautiful sunset you saw, a pleasant interaction, something delicious you ate, or something you did that you're proud of.

2. **Conduct a daily review:** Replay the three good things from the day after you identify them. Over time, your brain will start actively seeking out similar moments throughout the day.

3. **Post gratitude reminders:** Place visual reminders, such as sticky notes, in your environment to prompt you to pause and reflect on something you're grateful for.

These practices gradually rewire your brain, expanding your capacity to notice and appreciate the positive aspects of life. Starting a gratitude practice is an intentional effort to recalibrate your thinking patterns and cultivate a more balanced outlook so you can more fully appreciate life's positive aspects.

# Repeat Self-Compassion Statements
## Emotional Awareness, Literacy, and Resilience

Self-compassion doesn't come easily for many Autistic people, as it may appear abstract, potentially manipulative, or simply bewildering as a concept. This struggle is particularly prominent if you mask, as you often harbor a relentless inner critic whose goal is to shield you from potential humiliation. Your inner critic is trying to protect you from other people's shame by beating them to the punch. Essentially, it attempts to safeguard you from the beratement of others by self-shaming before they get the chance!

Since this inner critic acts both as a guardian and a source of pain, it can feel intimidating to try to silence it—it may feel like trying to hush a barking dog that could be warning you of impending danger. Attempting to silence this protective force can evoke a sense of threat, making self-compassion a complex endeavor!

If you find this struggle relatable, consider integrating self-compassion statements that tie you to the broader human experience and emphasize self-attunement. Steer clear of excessively sentimental self-compassion statements that may incite an internal conflict with your inner critic or your Autistic mask, which seeks approval from allistic people. Until you tackle internalized neurodivergent shame and ableism, engaging in self-compassion exercises may set off a fierce internal battle!

For example, I find statements like "I am free to disregard others' judgments," "I am deserving of kindness and compassion," and "I am worthy of love and acceptance" particularly challenging to embrace (which I suspect is largely due to my experiences in an ableist society and my dislike of overly emotional language). Instead, I turn to self-compassion statements that concentrate more on acknowledging my immediate experience and discomfort. This is a form of radical self-attunement, whereby I am gently present with the distressing moment confronting me.

Here are some more balanced self-compassion statements that I find easier to adopt.

If self-compassion proves challenging for you, try repeating mild statements like these:

- This is a difficult moment. This is painful.
- I'm not alone in this. Others have felt this way before too.
- I'm human, and it's okay to feel the way I do.
- It's okay to feel what I feel right now.
- I trust my capacity to grow and learn from this experience.
- I'm going to get through this. I've faced tough times before and survived.
- I'm doing the best I can with what I have right now, and that's enough.

You will be practicing a powerful form of self-compassion when you tune into yourself during painful moments and simply acknowledge their difficulty.

# Practice Affect Labeling
## *Emotional Regulation*

Managing and regulating emotions can be challenging for Autistic people. Sensory overload, heightened nervous systems, and other factors can make emotion regulation more taxing. We often have difficulty keeping our emotions within a tolerable threshold where we can effectively work through them. However, a simple yet powerful practice can help: affect labeling.

Research has shown that labeling your emotions in real time can help calm you down. A recent study showed how this works. Participants in the study (all of whom feared spiders) were divided into groups, exposed to a live spider, and given different instructions. The group that was told to simply acknowledge their emotional experience by stating their emotions had the most significant improvements. By identifying their feelings, they were able to regulate their anxiety and make progress in facing their fear.

Labeling emotions has a direct impact on your brain. It activates the prefrontal cortex, which plays a crucial role in emotional regulation. This activation helps calm the amygdala and the limbic system, reducing the intensity of emotional responses.

Practicing affect labeling is invaluable for cultivating resilience, particularly for Autistic people, who often struggle with emotion identification due to alexithymia. Our difficulty in recognizing emotions contributes to increased anxiety and stress. We can improve this skill by intentionally engaging in affect-labeling practices.

Here are some practices that can help enhance affect labeling:

- **Develop emotional awareness:** Take time to observe physical sensations, thoughts, and behaviors linked to different emotions. Additionally, consider incorporating interoception-building techniques to help you recognize patterns that indicate specific emotional states (refer to Tune Into Your Body's Signals with a Body Scan and Integrate Body Awareness Into Daily Activities in Chapter 2).

- **Utilize visual aids:** Visual aids, such as the emotion matrix and feeling wheel, can help you label emotions. These color-coded lists of words can give you the vocabulary to identify your feelings.

- **Track your moods:** Using a mood tracker worksheet or app can help you become more aware of your emotions and notice trends.

- **Practice mindfulness:** Develop mindfulness to increase your present-moment awareness of emotions. Mindfulness can help you develop a clearer understanding of your emotional landscape. (See the Resist Emotional Avoidance and Move Toward Acceptance entry in this chapter for more.)

- **Journal:** Write in a journal to reflect on your experiences, noting moments when you experience various emotions and describing associated sensations. This practice enhances your emotional-attunement skills and improves your ability to accurately label and understand your feelings.

- **Seek social support:** Talk to trusted friends or family members who can provide an understanding space for discussing emotions. Sharing emotional experiences and seeking feedback can enhance your emotional understanding and affect-labeling skills.

- **Talk to a therapist:** A therapist can help you process emotions in such a way as to increase your emotional insight and awareness of your emotional landscape.

By incorporating affect-labeling practices into your daily life, you can build emotional resilience while gaining a deeper understanding of your emotions.

# Distinguish Anxiety versus Sensory Overload

## Emotional Regulation

One of the crucial skills that can help Autistic people improve emotional regulation is recognizing the distinction between emotions and sensory overload. It's like untangling a knot, figuring out what's causing your distress and discomfort. If you can understand whether your feelings are rooted in your internal thoughts and emotions or triggered by external sensory stimuli, you can gain insight into how to better regulate your nervous system.

For example, navigating through a school or a store can be a challenging experience, with bright lights, loud noises, and crowded spaces bombarding your senses. You might feel overwhelmed and agitated. However, it is helpful to distinguish this sensory overload from the anxiety, fear, sadness, or anger that you may experience in response to specific situations or thoughts.

Sensory overload occurs when your senses are inundated with external stimuli, leading to heightened agitation and discomfort. In some cases, it may resemble anxiety and can contribute to angry outbursts and emotional dysregulation, making it difficult to differentiate between the two experiences.

**To differentiate between sensory overload and anxiety, pay attention to the triggers and physical sensations:**

- If your distress is primarily driven by external stimuli, such as loud noises, bright lights, or crowded environments, it is likely a result of sensory overload.

- If your distress is primarily driven by internal thoughts, worries, or emotional triggers, it is indicative of anxiety or other emotion-based experiences.

By developing this awareness, you can find the right self-care practices to navigate both your emotional experiences and sensory overload. For sensory overload, you can use sensory blockers—tools or techniques that help reduce sensory input, such as noise-canceling headphones or sunglasses—and take sensory breaks to give your nervous system a chance to calm down. When it comes to your emotions, you can employ emotional-regulation techniques.

Another critical distinction is learning the difference between anxiety (which is emotional) and sensory dread. As explained by Dr. Jonathan Dalton, licensed psychologist and founder and director of the Center for Anxiety and Behavioral Change, anxiety is the fear of potential future events driven by internal thoughts—differing from dread, which is the anticipation of known discomfort. Sensory dread, often experienced by Autistic individuals, is the fear of known situations that can cause sensory overload. For example, you may feel sensory dread when anticipating visits to the mall, dentist, or grocery store, as you know these environments likely cause sensory overload.

Both anxiety and sensory dread can cause you to avoid certain situations. Sensory dread may lead you to avoid known sensory-rich situations. In contrast, anxiety may lead you to avoid getting together with a friend or going to a job interview due to fear of potential embarrassment or negative judgment.

When confronted with sensory dread, it can be helpful to prepare yourself in advance by using sensory blockers, having an exit plan to take sensory breaks, and limiting the amount of high-sensory tasks in your day. For anxiety, you can try unhooking from unhelpful thoughts, practicing relaxation techniques, and challenging avoidance patterns.

Understanding the differences between your emotions and sensory overload allows you to respond with greater self-awareness and take targeted actions to regulate yourself. It's like having a road map to guide you through the twists and turns of your inner world.

# Harness the Power
# of Effective Worrying
## *Emotional Regulation*

Worry often gets a bad reputation, but it can serve a purpose. Worrying allows you to anticipate potential challenges, analyze risks, and problem-solve. However, when worry becomes overwhelming and consumes your thoughts, it can negatively impact your emotional well-being. The key is to worry effectively and productively. (Yes, that *is* possible.)

One strategy for managing worry is to create a designated "Worry Period." This dedicated time allows you to contain your worries and address them in a structured and intentional way.

Implementing a Worry Period involves these steps:

1. Choose a designated time: Select a consistent time slot each day for your Worry Period (around 10–20 minutes). This will be the time when you dedicate your full attention to addressing worries.

2. Write down your worries: Use a notebook or digital tool to jot down worries. Externalizing thoughts creates a sense of containment.

3. Break worries into tasks: As you list your worries, distinguish between those you can control (within your circle of influence, meaning you can take actions that influence the outcome) and those you cannot. For the worries within your control, create actionable steps to address each concern. Transforming your worries into concrete actions makes them more manageable.

4. Practice mindfulness: When worries arise during the day, remind your mind that you will address them during the designated Worry Period.

Remember, worry can actually be productive if you manage it intentionally. This Worry Period can help you regain control over your concerns as you identify them and break them down into tasks that can address their sources.

# Uncover Your Raw Spots and Triggers
## *Emotional Regulation*

Raw spots are sensitive areas that can evoke strong emotional reactions within you. They represent vulnerabilities and past wounds that, when brought to the surface unexpectedly, intensify your emotions. When your raw spots are triggered, your past experiences intrude into the present, causing you to respond not only to the immediate stressor but also to your historical pain.

Identifying raw spots enhances your understanding of your emotional reactions and enables you to take better control of these moments.

To increase awareness of your raw spots:

- **Reflect on past experiences:** Consider situations that have triggered strong emotional responses. Document triggering events, including the context, your reactions, and associated thoughts. Look for patterns and themes over time.

- **Notice reactions:** Pay attention to how your body and mind react when encountering potential triggers. Be mindful of physical sensations and emotions.

- **Identify the story:** Raw spots are often connected to stories we tell ourselves. These stories can be deeply ingrained, influencing how you view yourself, others, and the world.

Once you've identified your raw spots, develop strategies to manage them. For example, you might mindfully acknowledge and name your raw spots when they are activated (such as, "My abandonment fear is activated right now"), seek support from trusted people, and employ relaxation techniques like deep-breathing exercises or progressive muscle relaxation to reduce emotional distress.

# Find Alternatives to Self-Harm
## *Emotional Regulation*

Self-harm can manifest as a coping response for many Autistic people, often arising from various factors such as overwhelming sensory experiences, an attempt to cope with intense emotions, the need for sensory input, or an urge to punish ourselves. Self-harm can also become addictive due to a complex interplay of factors, including the temporary relief or distraction it provides, the release of endorphins that can induce a sense of euphoria, and the underlying emotional distress that drives it.

By taking a harm-reduction approach, we can cultivate alternative strategies that provide healthier ways to cope with difficult emotions.

Here are some alternative activities to try:

- **Grab ice:** Holding ice or doing an ice dive (putting your face in ice water) for up to twenty seconds or safely placing an ice pack on your body can provide a jolt of cold sensation. This can release endorphins and create a similar physiological response to self-harm but with less risk involved.

- **Practice grounding techniques:** Grounding techniques help redirect your attention away from distressing thoughts (see the Anchor in the Present Moment entry in this chapter for more).

- **Try changing temperatures:** Alternating between warm and cold temperatures, such as taking a warm shower followed by a splash of cold water, can stimulate the body and shift your focus away from distress. Temperature changes also impact the body's physiological responses, including increasing blood flow and releasing endorphins (not recommended if you have dysautonomia, such as POTS).

- **Move—and quickly:** Engaging in rapid movement, such as running, dancing, or jumping, can increase your heart rate and stimulate the release of endorphins. These activities help channel emotional energy into a more constructive outlet.

- **Soothe your senses:** Engage in self-care practices that comfort and relax you. This could include taking a warm bath, listening to calming music, or doing activities that bring you joy and relaxation. These activities can help regulate emotions and promote a sense of well-being.

- **Use a TENS unit:** A TENS (Transcutaneous Electrical Nerve Stimulation) unit, is a device that delivers low-voltage electrical currents through electrodes placed on the skin. It can be a helpful tool if sensory dysregulation is contributing to self-harming behaviors, as it provides a strong sensory input that can assist in sensory regulation and provide relief. (While TENS units can be used on your own at home, consult with a health care provider before using one, especially if you have any underlying medical conditions such as epilepsy, and be sure to attend to safety precautions when using it.)

- **Seek support:** Reach out to trusted friends, family members, or mental health professionals who can provide understanding, validation, and support during difficult times.

- **Assemble a distress-tolerance kit:** Assemble a collection of items that provide comfort and distraction during distressing moments. This could include stress balls, fidget toys, soothing lotions, a picture of a loved one, a meaningful note, or a favorite book. Having a distress-tolerance kit allows you to quickly access healthy coping tools so you don't turn to self-harm.

You can strengthen your response to overwhelming emotions and situations with these tips—but don't be afraid to ask for help too. Self-harm is a serious matter, and you may need professional support for managing it.

# Anchor in the Present Moment
## *Emotional Regulation*

Grounding techniques are akin to a sturdy anchor that can hold you steadfastly through the turbulent waves of intense emotions. Just as an anchor keeps a boat in one place amid a stormy sea, grounding techniques provide you with a reliable touchstone when you are faced with overwhelming emotions, anxiety, panic, dissociation, or a sense of disconnection from the present moment.

In those challenging times, grounding techniques help you find stability, regain a sense of presence, and navigate your inner experiences with greater clarity and resilience. Grounding techniques also moor you in the present moment, establishing a firm connection to reality and enhancing your overall well-being.

Here are some ideas to try anchoring yourself in the present moment:

- **Physical grounding techniques:** These methods involve bringing your attention to your body and the sensations you experience. Physical grounding can include practices such as running cool water over your hands and focusing on the sensation, or engaging in gentle physical movements. By focusing on the physical sensations, you anchor yourself in the present moment and create a sense of stability and grounding.

- **Mental grounding techniques:** Mental grounding involves redirecting your thoughts. This can be done through activities like counting, reciting mantras, and engaging in cognitive distractions, such as solving puzzles. You can also try giving your mind specific tasks, like identifying cities that start with the letter "P" or recalling songs by a certain artist. These activities serve to distract you from the distressing thoughts. By shifting your attention, you cultivate a sense of mental stability, allowing you to regain control.

- **Sensory grounding techniques:** These techniques engage your senses to connect with the immediate environment. This can be achieved by focusing on sensory experiences, such as listening to calming music, feeling the texture of an object, or smelling a soothing scent. Another effective technique is the 5-4-3-2-1 sensory grounding exercise: Identify five things you can see, four things you can touch or feel, three things you can hear, two things you can smell, and one thing you can taste. By immersing yourself in the present sensory experience, you will also ground yourself in the present moment.

Grounding techniques support you as you manage overwhelming emotions and restore a sense of balance from which you can then process those emotions. One important note: Grounding techniques should not be used as a long-term strategy to avoid your painful emotions. Emotional avoidance is not helpful in the long run. These techniques are most effective as temporary tools for navigating intense emotions and bringing you back to a space from which you can effectively process your emotions.

# Resist Emotional Avoidance and Move Toward Acceptance
## Emotional Regulation

I used to refer to my emotions as those "pesky little things." I consider myself an emotion minimizer, which I used to chalk up to being a highly analytical and logically oriented person. And while this is certainly a part of it, I have realized a negative (or shadow) side to my relationship with emotions. In addition to being an emotion minimizer, I am also prone to emotional avoidance. And it has taken an active effort to unlearn my ways!

Emotional avoidance is a common coping mechanism among many Autistic people. When you suppress or avoid feelings due to fear or discomfort, you're unfortunately vulnerable to substance abuse, addiction, self-harm, and emotional numbing. Additionally, emotional avoidance heightens stress, anxiety, and disconnection from yourself and others, potentially contributing to chronic pain or other physical complaints. Moreover, it impairs your problem-solving abilities and hampers effective resolution of underlying issues.

For Autistic people, the inclination toward emotional avoidance is understandable. Many of us develop this in response to the too-muchness of the world—the overwhelming sensory experiences and challenges we face in processing and expressing emotions. While emotional avoidance may provide temporary relief, it can have long-term detrimental effects on your mental health.

When you embrace emotional acceptance, you cultivate positive coping mechanisms to acknowledge and engage with your emotions. It means granting permission for emotions to run their natural course. Positive coping skills include any methods where you are actively processing and working through your emotions.

Here are some examples of positive coping:

- **Journaling:** Writing down your thoughts and feelings can be a powerful tool for emotional exploration and processing. Through journaling, you can gain insights into your emotions, identify patterns or triggers, and find clarity in your experiences.

- **Mindfulness:** Mindfulness practices involve bringing your attention to the present moment with curiosity and nonjudgment. Observing your thoughts and feelings without attaching to them or getting carried away can help you develop a more balanced and gentle relationship with your emotional experiences.

- **Therapy:** Therapy allows you to work with a trained professional who can support you in exploring and processing your emotions. Therapists can help you develop coping strategies and gain insight into your emotions.

- **Emotional expression:** Engaging in creative outlets, such as art or music, allows you to express and explore your emotions cathartically. Creating art or playing music can provide a sense of release and offer communication when words are difficult to find.

Emotional acceptance requires self-awareness and compassion. It involves recognizing that all emotions, including discomfort, provide valuable insights. By accepting and approaching your emotions with curiosity and kindness, you cultivate resilience and self-awareness to navigate life's challenges.

# CHAPTER FOUR

• • •

# Mental Self-Care

Did you know that the majority of Autistic people are likely to encounter some mental health condition in their lifetimes? Research suggests that conditions such as anxiety, depression, PTSD, and OCD are especially prevalent among Autistic people. These facts underscore how essential it is to take care of your mental health.

Tending to our mental well-being with kindness and compassion is one way of cultivating greater mental health resilience. By understanding and unraveling the complexities of your Autistic mind, you can harness its strengths and brainstorm tactics to navigate its susceptibilities.

Caring for your mental health can encompass a variety of practices, from seeking a supportive therapist to cultivating a healthy relationship with your thoughts and honing your self-advocacy skills. This chapter features an array of self-care activities specifically customized to help you work with your Autistic brain instead of against it. You'll find sections on how to embrace your Autistic identity and interests, advocate for your mental health care, understand your Autistic mindset and well-being, and build mental health resilience. Activities include strategies for integrating your neurodivergent identity, noticing negative narratives and changing the script, finding a neurodivergent-affirming therapist, and more. These ideas are geared toward empowering you to build resilience, foster self-acceptance, and devise effective strategies for managing your mental health.

Tending to your mental health is not a reflection of weakness but a bold act of self-advocacy. By engaging in these self-care practices, you are not only prioritizing your well-being but also fostering your overall mental health as an Autistic person.

# Celebrate Your Neurodivergent Identity
## *Autistic Identity and Interests*

Celebrating your neurodivergent identity is built on loving yourself just as you are. Everyone tends to relegate to the shadows parts of themselves that evoke shame, concealing them away, and Autistic people are no different. But celebrating your Autistic identity is a courageous act—an opportunity to unabashedly embrace the essence of who you are.

The process of celebrating your identity will take a unique form for you, as it does for each person. For me, it entails connecting with Autistic culture; embracing identity-first language, declaring proudly, "I am Autistic"; and acknowledging that autism is interwoven into the fabric of my being and is a vital aspect of my identity that I am unashamedly proud of.

You might use some of the same methods I do, or you may choose to express your neurodivergent identity in other ways. You might opt for visible displays, such as wearing clothing or accessories with symbols like the infinity logo, the neuroqueer pride flag, or the sunflower logo, or maybe you'll celebrate your autism through artistic pursuits or personal advocacy.

By celebrating your neurodivergent identity, you are creating a narrative that authentically reflects your lived experience. This isn't a one-time celebration; it is an ongoing, daily journey of self-discovery and self-acceptance. Embrace your personal strength and own your neurodivergent identity in whatever way feels natural to you.

# Address Internalized Ableism
## Autistic Identity and Interests

"Ableism" refers to discrimination or devaluation of someone based on their physical, mental, intellectual, or other disability. Internalized ableism is the way that a person with a disability absorbs (even unconsciously) this harmful mindset. Internalized ableism is similar to internalized racism and internalized homophobia in that all those groups are absorbing negative messages about their communities on a daily basis, and then they encounter emotional or physical damage as a result.

Sometimes ableist messages are subtle, like when someone diminishes your effort and says things like "You're just being lazy" or discounts your sensory experiences by insisting that you're "overreacting." Other times you might encounter overt ableist incidents, such as people using derogatory terms or making fun of disabled people. If you hold multiple marginalized identities, you are likely navigating a complex web of internalized isms and are subjected to several layers of harmful messages on a regular basis. These toxic messages and internalized criticisms have a direct impact on both your emotional and physical health. While the process can be difficult, working to recognize and undo the damage they cause is an important facet of mental self-care.

If you find yourself descending into a neurodivergent shame spiral, take a moment to scan your thoughts and see if internalized ableism might be at the root. For instance, after experiencing an awkward social interaction or struggling to keep up with neurotypical expectations and pace of life, I used to berate myself, thinking, "Why can't you be like others? So-and-so can do it effortlessly. It's not that difficult." Now I catch these thoughts and recognize them for what they are: internalized ableism in action. Whenever we hold ourselves to neurotypical standards and condemn ourselves for not meeting them, we are experiencing internalized ableism in action.

Here are some other examples of instances of internalized ableism to watch for:

- **Self-doubt:** Doubting your abilities solely based on being Autistic, such as thinking, "I can't handle this task because I'm Autistic."
- **Apologizing for neurodivergent behaviors:** Feeling the need to apologize for behaviors that are natural expressions of neurodivergence, like saying, "Sorry for rambling" or "I'm sorry for being awkward."
- **Masking or camouflaging:** Adopting neurotypical behaviors or suppressing natural Autistic traits in order to fit in—for example, consciously mimicking neurotypical social norms or suppressing stimming.
- **Internalized stereotypes:** Believing negative stereotypes or societal misconceptions about autism, leading to negative self-perceptions.

If you recognize any of these examples happening to you, pause and ask yourself:

- "Is internalized ableism influencing this thought?"
- "Am I imposing neurotypical standards upon myself?"
- "What would I tell my Autistic friend (or child) in this moment?"

Bringing your awareness to this ableism is the first step in beginning to dismantle it emotionally. You have the power to challenge these negative thoughts and instead foster self-compassion, embrace your neurodivergent identity, and love yourself just as you are!

# Drop "Functioning" Labels
## *Autistic Identity and Interests*

One way we can work together to provide care to the Autistic community (and, in turn, self-care) is to nix the habit of applying "functioning" labels. Imagine if neurotypical people were asked their "functioning" levels—it would seem rude and judgmental. So why are we doing it to Autistic people?

Functioning labels also fail to capture the intricate complexities of people's skills and behaviors. For example, my functioning fluctuates greatly depending on my sensory environment, my level of burnout, and the energy expended on socializing and masking. Clearly, functioning levels exist on a fluid spectrum—which they do for most people!

Functioning labels also dismiss the challenges of Autistic people who mask, while simultaneously diminishing the strengths of nonspeaking Autistic people who possess rich inner worlds and have much to offer society.

Instead of relying on functioning labels, try to self-advocate by shifting the focus to support needs. This shift changes the conversation from how well you function to considering what supports can help you thrive. For example, someone with level 3 autism will require higher levels of support, so the focus should be on discussing their needs and the needs of their families who provide daily support. Individuals with level 1 autism may have fewer intensive daily living-support needs but tend to have high mental health support needs and benefit from specific mental health and sensory supports.

By reframing this conversation from functioning labels to support needs, we move beyond the limitations of functioning labels and redirect the conversation toward the vital supports that empower us to flourish.

# Spend Time Unmasked
## *Autistic Identity and Interests*

Many Autistic traits are actually innate strategies we use to calm our bodies. For example, avoiding eye contact helps calm the amygdala (the brain's fear/emotion center), and engaging in stimming helps regulate senses. However, those of us who mask our Autistic traits suppress these natural instincts that regulate our bodies and brains. No wonder many of us are burned out and struggling with our mental health—we are overriding our natural self-soothing mechanisms! If you instead intentionally spend time unmasking, you can relax and enjoy behaviors that naturally support and soothe you.

Masking also involves contorting your communication to fit in with the dominant culture. Translating Autistic speech to allistic speech takes a lot of energy from your prefrontal cortex (the front part of your brain, in charge of thinking and decision-making). It turns out that your brain needs to work really hard to translate your direct, efficient Autistic speech into indirect, nonefficient allistic speech!

When you unmask your communication, you give yourself permission to speak directly and candidly, embrace divergent conversations, and skip the small talk that can be so draining. It's a powerful brain break that can help you recharge and feel more centered.

The next time you're feeling burned out, it might be because you're drained from masking. To recharge, find a safe space to unmask, either with other Autistic people, a trusted friend or family member, or simply on your own. Just ensure you're in a safe space to do so. Your body and your brain will thank you for it.

# Welcome Autistic Stimming
## *Autistic Identity and Interests*

Stimming is a natural and comforting behavior many Autistic people engage in. It can take many forms, from hand flapping to twirling to rocking back and forth to auditory or vocal stimming, where the person repeats a song or makes repetitive sounds. While stimming might seem strange or even concerning to some non-Autistic people, it is an integral part of many Autistic people's experience.

One of the reasons Autistic people stim is because it helps soothe our sensory systems. The extra sensory input that stimming provides can be helpful when we're feeling overloaded, overwhelmed, or even excited by our environment. Stimming is our brain's way of helping us out when things get overwhelming—it is like our personal tool kit for dealing with sensory overload.

Here are some benefits of stimming:

- **It redirects attention:** Stimming helps us tune out the clutter around us because we focus on a sensory activity we enjoy.

- **It provides control and homeostasis:** When in overwhelming environments, stimming helps us focus on sensory stuff we can control and provides enough input to help us block out what we can't control. Stimming provides a sense of predictability and mastery in an otherwise unpredictable environment. Additionally, it creates a sense of homeostasis, offering comfort and security. You know what's coming when you stim, and that can be comforting when navigating an unpredictable situation!

- **It feels soothing:** Actions like rocking and tapping can be really calming—partly because it may influence our brain chemistry! Engaging in stimming activities may increase dopamine, glutamate, and aspartate, which can lead to a sense of calm and relaxation, making us feel relaxed.

- **It satisfies sensory seekers:** Stimming can also be a form of sensory seeking. Sometimes, our environment doesn't give us the sensory input we crave. Stimming helps us get the comfort we need.

And there's even more good news! Research suggests that stimming, particularly rhythmic movements like rocking and swaying, may actually release endorphins in the brain. These feel-good chemicals can help boost your mood and reduce feelings of pain and discomfort.

If you're an Autistic person who stims, know that you're not alone and there's nothing wrong with you. Stimming is a valuable and important part of who you are! Embrace your sensory needs and find the stims that work best for you. Whether it's pacing, stim dancing, hand flapping, twirling your hair, or tapping your foot, your body knows what it needs to feel calm and comfortable. So stim on!

# Regulate Emotions Through Movement
## Autistic Identity and Interests

In high school, even before I knew I was Autistic, I engaged in all sorts of rhythmic activities. I would come home from school and go on long Rollerblade rides with Spice Girls playing on my Walkman. And at night I'd dance it out behind closed doors to the best music the nineties had to offer.

It turns out my interest in music and dancing may have been partly related to my autism. Autistic people thrive on repetitive, rhythmic movement. Autistic bodies tend to generate excess energy and benefit from releasing that energy at the end of the day. When we don't find a way to release this energy, it tends to sneak out through emotional or sensory meltdowns!

That's where rhythmic movement comes in—it's one of the most powerful tools in our mental health tool kit! If dancing isn't your thing, you can find other rhythmic activities that work for you, like pacing, bouncing on a yoga ball, jumping, or Rollerblading.

Rhythmic movement not only lets you release pent-up energy and emotions; it also helps you connect with your body in a positive way. It's a way to bring your attention out of your head and into the positive sensations of your body. This can be grounding and help you feel more present and anchored in the moment. When you're more grounded in your body, you're more easily able to connect to your mental experience.

Dancing also stimulates a beneficial surge of dopamine, your body's "feel-good" neurotransmitter! Additionally, it helps lower levels of cortisol, a hormone associated with stress (which is often high in Autistic people).

So whether you're dancing it out or engaging in other rhythmic activities, take some time to connect with your body and notice the physical sensations. With practice, you may just find it easier to embrace the positive aspects of having a body.

# Identify Your Values
## *Autistic Identity and Interests*

Autistic people tend to be very value driven. After all, values are woven into the fabric of your identity, shaping how you see yourself and the world around you. When you find yourself in situations that conflict with your values, it can be emotionally draining and create inner turmoil. On the other hand, when you are aligned with your values and doing things that reflect who you are and what you care about, it brings a sense of clarity and purpose to your life and helps you feel anchored in your authentic self.

Identifying your values is a good first step toward living a life that is in sync with them. As a reflection exercise, take a moment to list out your top five values. They could be political ideals, personal passions, or anything else that matters deeply to you.

Here are examples of values:

- Equality and inclusivity
- Curiosity and learning
- Autonomy and independence
- Creativity
- Authenticity
- Animal rights
- Personal growth
- Spirituality
- Sustainability

Alternatively, if you online search for "value card sort," you'll find online versions of this exercise that provide more guidance and structure.

When you're feeling disconnected from yourself, consider connecting with one of your values through an activity that resonates with it. By doing so, you are aligning with your core self.

Your values are not just things you have—they are integral to who you are. Embracing your values is one way of embracing and celebrating your Autistic identity. Consciously living in sync with your foundational values is an effective way to take care of your body, mind, and spirit.

# Celebrate Your Special Interests
## *Autistic Identity and Interests*

My brain works in self-contained worlds that I refer to as "ecosystems." I see connections, links, patterns, and relations in everything. When I become passionate about something, I must understand it in its entirety. This is what I call the "special interest ecosystem." This might sound familiar to you, because approaching interests in this deep way is actually a common trait of Autistic people.

My special interest ecosystem has become a crucial part of my self-care routine. When I'm feeling overwhelmed or stressed, I turn to my interests for comfort and grounding because they provide a sense of stability and familiarity.

Your interests not only are deeply integrated into your identity but also can be incredibly soothing. They can help you reduce stress, emotionally regulate, and access a wellspring of energy to help you feel more grounded. You can find comfort and safety in the deep understanding you have about your areas of interest. As a bonus, connecting with other people about your areas of interest is a powerful way to forge and strengthen connections and relationships.

However, many Autistic people resist leaning into their special interests. Society often views these interests as abnormal or obsessive, which can lead to internalized shame and embarrassment. This mindset can make it challenging to embrace the power of your special interest energy for self-soothing.

Try flipping the script on any negative associations you may have with your interests and celebrate them instead. After all, the energy behind special interests can drive innovation, creativity, and social change. Many groundbreaking inventions and movements have come from people deeply passionate about particular subjects. For example, Greta Thunberg's interest in environmental justice has ignited a spark within millions, inspiring them to rally against the threat of climate collapse. Similarly, Steve Jobs, cofounder of Apple, was known for his obsession with the convergence of technology and design, which reshaped the technological landscape. (Note: While Jobs exhibited numerous Autistic traits, there is no definitive evidence to confirm he was Autistic.)

Because interests and identity are so interwoven for Autistic people, embracing your interests is a form of embracing your identity. You will cultivate a strong sense of self through your interests, making them a foundational part of your mental self-care.

To integrate special interests into self-care, consider reserving specific time for delving into your passions, using your interests as emotional-regulation tools, weaving your hobbies into daily activities, or leveraging them to cultivate social connections. See what resonates with you—the key is to not be ashamed of your level of interest. By embracing these interests and incorporating them into your self-care routine, you can find a sense of stability and familiarity in a world that often feels overwhelming and unpredictable.

# Build and Cooperate with Your Health Care Team
## *Self-Advocacy in Mental Health Care*

Establishing a collaborative relationship with your health care team, including prescribers and primary care providers, is a cornerstone for navigating your mental health as an Autistic person. This partnership not only puts your distinct medical needs front of mind but also supports adept management of any necessary medications. (Note: While there is no prescribed medication specifically for autism, many Autistic individuals benefit from therapeutic pharmaceutical intervention to manage co-occurring conditions such as anxiety, depression, ADHD, PTSD, OCD, and others.)

For many Autistic people, navigating the health care industry can be overwhelming due to various challenges, including sensory sensitivities, executive functioning challenges, communication differences, and frequent medical visits due to co-occurring conditions. Therefore, it's a powerful act of self-care to develop a collaborative relationship with your medical team.

Here are some strategies for forging such relationships:

- **Identify autism-informed professionals:** Try to find health care practitioners who are experienced in caring for Autistic people and knowledgeable about autism's intricacies. They should understand common co-occurring conditions, sensory sensitivities, and potential medication interactions affecting Autistic individuals.

- **Get recommendations from Autistic communities:** Recommendations from local or online Autistic communities can provide potential leads to Autistic-affirming providers. Autism advocacy organizations might also have lists of providers.

- **Foster an open dialogue:** Make it a point to communicate your concerns, needs, and goals. Take an active role in sharing essential details about your sensory sensitivities, pain, and medication history and any side effects you experience. It's important to note that Autistic people tend to be more sensitive to medication and may experience medication side effects more frequently than their non-Autistic counterparts. Also, the ways Autistic people express distress or discomfort can be different from allistic expectations, which can sometimes lead to misinterpretation by providers. Thus, maintaining open communication is vital to ensuring your symptoms are correctly understood and addressed.

- **Write down your concerns:** If you find yourself flustered during medical visits, prepare ahead by jotting down critical points or questions. This helps ensure you articulate your concerns effectively and can aid your self-advocacy efforts.

- **Consider recording your appointments:** If it's challenging to remember visit details, ask if you can audio record the session for later reference, particularly if instructions are being shared.

- **Advocate for regular monitoring:** Regular health check-ins and medication management are crucial, particularly considering the heightened likelihood of medication side effects. Teletherapy can offer an accessible alternative with fewer sensory concerns for these ongoing assessments or nonemergency consultations.

- **Join in the decision-making process:** Engage actively in your health care decisions. Understand the potential benefits and risks of proposed treatments, and collaborate with your provider in making informed choices.

Ideally, you will be able to find a health care professional who is knowledgeable about autism. In situations where autism-informed providers are not available, finding a provider who at least takes a collaborative approach and who is open to learning about autism can go a long way!

# Address Co-occurring Mental Health Conditions
## *Self-Advocacy in Mental Health Care*

It's important to underscore that autism, a form of neurodivergence, is not in and of itself a condition that warrants treatment. However, many Autistic people face co-occurring mental health conditions that, if unmanaged, can significantly affect their well-being. Treating these coexisting conditions is really important for maintaining good mental health.

Co-occurring mental health conditions can include anxiety, depression, PTSD, OCD, and other conditions. Furthermore, many Autistic individuals also experience other forms of neurodivergence, including ADHD and dyslexia, that benefit from targeted support. These coexisting conditions and forms of neurodivergence can amplify daily life challenges and impact the mental health of Autistic people.

Here are some strategies to navigate mental health care effectively:

- Explore personalized management of co-occurring conditions: There is a myriad of therapeutic approaches available to address co-occurring conditions, such as acceptance and commitment therapy (ACT), dialectical behavior therapy (DBT), Internal Family Systems (IFS), somatic-based therapies, and trauma-focused therapy. Each of these therapies offers strategies to tackle specific challenges. While there's no "one-size-fits-all" therapy for Autistic people due to our broad diversity, many of us respond well to somatic-based therapies, relational and interpersonal therapies, and IFS. Traditional cognitive behavioral therapy (CBT) may not suit all of us, with ACT and DBT often providing beneficial alternatives for those seeking structured approaches.

- **Find a neurodivergent-affirming therapist:** Neurodivergent-affirming therapists think of autism as a valid part of your identity (versus a disorder to fix). Finding a therapist who values your autism as a part of your identity and will help you integrate it into your sense of self and work through internalized shame, neurodivergent trauma, and more is a powerful investment in your mental health (see Find a Neurodivergent-Affirming Provider in this chapter for tips on what to look for).

- **Consider pharmacological intervention:** In some instances, medication can alleviate symptoms of coexisting conditions. Develop a collaborative relationship with a psychiatrist or prescribing health care professional to ensure appropriate medication prescription and effective monitoring (see Build and Cooperate with Your Health Care Team in this chapter for more tips on cultivating a collaborative relationship with your prescriber).

- **Develop coping mechanisms:** Learning and implementing coping strategies enhances your ability to manage symptoms and navigate daily life. Strategies can include stress-management techniques, nervous system regulation strategies, emotional-regulation skills, sensory self-care practices, and mindfulness. You can find lots of ideas in this book to get you started, then a therapist can offer additional guidance.

- **Connect with supportive communities:** Getting in touch with supportive communities, both online and offline, can foster a sense of understanding and belonging. Your engagement with neurodivergent groups or networks can provide valuable resources, validation, and support.

Addressing co-occurring mental health conditions is a way to commit to prioritizing your mental health while empowering yourself to flourish and thrive.

# Find a Neurodivergent-Affirming Provider
## Self-Advocacy in Mental Health Care

Identifying a mental health professional who will respect and advocate for neurodivergence can be a pivotal element of your mental health journey. To assist in this pursuit, consider the following green and red flags during your search:

## GREEN FLAGS

Look for "green flags," or indications that a health care provider embraces and validates neurodivergence, such as:

- **Inclusive language:** Professionals who use identity-first language (e.g., "Autistic" versus "has autism" or "with autism") when discussing autism and neurodivergence convey respect and understanding of Autistic culture and people.

- **Affirmation of neurodiversity:** Look for providers who openly affirm neurodiversity and explicitly state their commitment to respect and celebrate neurodivergent identities.

- **Culturally competent care:** Professionals employing an intersectional framework to understand the experiences and challenges of intersecting identities—such as being Autistic and a member of another marginalized community—are likely to offer more nuanced and comprehensive care.

- **Emphasis on autonomy and agency:** Therapists who stress your autonomy, choice, and agency in treatment decisions respect you as an active participant in your health care journey.

- **Accessibility:** Providers who proactively make their practices more accessible—for instance, by offering flexible scheduling options, providing accommodations for sensory sensitivities, and using alternative communication methods—demonstrate practical understanding of the needs of Autistic clients.

## RED FLAGS

On the other hand, be very wary if you see any of these potential "red flags":

- **Emphasis on applied behavior analysis (ABA):** While ABA is a commonly recommended therapy, its focus on compliance can be detrimental to Autistic individuals. A provider heavily promoting or exclusively recommending ABA often does not align with neurodivergent perspectives.

- **Use of pathologizing language:** Be attentive to the language used by health care professionals when discussing autism. Frequent use of terms like "autism spectrum disorder (ASD)" or other pathologizing language may indicate an approach focused on treating autism as a problem to be fixed rather than recognizing it as an integral aspect of human neurodiversity.

- **"Fix-it" mentality:** Be cautious of health care professionals who often discuss "curing autism" or "improving social skills." If a provider suggests that the aim of treatment is to make an individual more "neurotypical," they are operating from a deficit-based framework— in other words, assuming that something about you needs to be "fixed." This mindset overlooks the value of neurodiversity, emphasizing "fixing" perceived issues rather than fostering personal growth and well-being within an individual's unique neurological context.

You can also turn to resources like Neurodivergent Therapists (NDTherapists.com), the Association of Neurodivergent Therapists (which is a UK directory), Therapy Den, and Inclusive Therapists to provide directories of therapists identifying as neurodivergent or affirming neurodivergent identities.

Lastly, trust your instincts. If you don't feel understood, respected, or comfortable during your initial interaction with a provider, it may be worthwhile to extend your search. Take your time, conduct thorough research, and prioritize your mental and physical well-being throughout this process. Finding the right fit is key to successful therapy, so it's worth your time and effort.

# Explore the Benefits and Drawbacks of Formal Diagnosis
## *Self-Advocacy in Mental Health Care*

Navigating your neurology is a deeply personal undertaking. For many Autistic people, seeking a formal diagnosis marks a significant milestone in our quest for enhanced mental well-being. However, this is often a mixed experience with benefits and challenges. Your experiences, resources, and societal factors will influence this process. While a formal diagnosis can be a powerful tool, Autistic identity transcends medical labels and flourishes instead in the community's richness of diversity, unique strengths, and personal experiences. If a formal diagnosis is on your radar, it's a good idea to weigh its potential advantages and disadvantages.

### Benefits of Diagnosis

- **Validation and self-understanding:** A formal diagnosis can offer a sense of validation. It can provide an explanation for lifelong struggles and differences and bring you enhanced self-understanding and a clearer sense of your identity. It can also bring about relief and empowerment, enabling you to advocate more effectively for yourself.

- **Access to resources and supports:** A formal diagnosis often serves as a gateway to specialized support and services. This could include therapies, educational and work accommodations, disability services, and potential financial aid.

## Drawbacks of Diagnosis

- **Pathologizing:** The medical model of disability often pathologizes neurodivergent identities. A formal diagnosis can sometimes foster a perception of being "disordered" or "deficient," potentially affecting self-esteem and overall well-being.

- **Accessibility and cost:** Gaining access to a formal diagnosis can be a hurdle due to factors such as geographic location, availability of specialists, and financial barriers. The diagnostic process can be costly and time-consuming, often with extended waitlists.

- **Potential stigma:** Despite increasing societal acceptance, the stigma associated with autism still persists. A diagnosis can sometimes lead to prejudiced attitudes, discrimination, and exclusion in various settings, including schools and workplaces.

- **Misdiagnosis:** Unfortunately, some clinicians have yet to update their understanding of autism, adhering instead to outdated stereotypes. As a result, if you are a woman, genderqueer, or a person of color, or if you deviate from the stereotypical autism profile, you may navigate the diagnostic process only to face the risk of being misdiagnosed.

- **Migration limitations:** Certain countries impose restrictions on immigration for individuals with an autism diagnoses, which could limit opportunities for international living.

- **Medical disparities:** In some cases, having a diagnosis of autism can potentially influence medical decision-making processes, such as organ transplant eligibility or access to gender-affirming care, due to misconceptions about the capacity and quality of life of Autistic individuals.

The decision to seek an autism diagnosis is deeply personal and should be tailored to your individual needs, circumstances, and preferences. Regardless of whether you pursue a formal diagnosis, remember that your experiences and identity as an Autistic person are valid. You have the right to understand yourself, advocate for your needs, and seek acceptance and respect.

# Reframe Your Autistic Childhood Experiences
## Autistic Mindset and Well-Being

A meaningful part of embracing your Autistic identity can be journeying back to your past, particularly your childhood, to reconsider and reinterpret those experiences through a new lens. Your history probably includes stories of your Autistic traits being misinterpreted, misunderstood, or even wrongly labeled as "character flaws" by yourself or others. Consequently, your self-perception and memories might be clouded by a sense of otherness, bewilderment, confusion, and shame.

As you deepen your grasp of your Autistic identity, you can reframe your past with newfound understanding. If you were once seen as being an isolated "loner," you can now understand that alone time is the manifestation of enjoyment of your rich inner landscape. Your aversions to specific textures or sounds, once deemed "picky" or "overreactive," were, in fact, your sensory system interacting with the world in a uniquely Autistic way. Your perceived "rudeness" was just your way of being direct, honest, and transparent. Those meltdowns were your body's natural response to sensory overload. Your passion—far from being "too much"—was a beautiful testament to your value-driven and passionate way of being in the world.

Reframing your narrative with this newfound lens can be a transformative mental health exercise. You are not "broken" or "flawed"; you simply perceive and interact with the world uniquely. Embracing your Autistic identity allows you to view your past self with compassion, appreciating the strength it took to navigate a world that didn't understand you. This process can cultivate empathy for the misunderstood child you once were while honoring the resilience that propelled you to where you are today.

# Forgive Yourself
## *Autistic Mindset and Well-Being*

People often ask how my late-in-life diagnosis has impacted me. My initial response usually revolves around one significant aspect: the awakening of self-compassion. My diagnosis essentially granted me permission to quiet my inner critic and extend kindness toward myself—a newfound experience. Through the lens of understanding my Autistic identity, I can finally release the perception of my "faults" that I once carried, cultivate a mindset of gentleness and self-forgiveness for past mistakes, and embrace realistic expectations for my future.

Reframing your narrative in a similar way will allow you to view your past self with greater gentleness. In addition to having self-compassion for your Autistic traits and limits, which you may have misinterpreted as character flaws, it's important to recognize that there may be other aspects for which you need to offer yourself forgiveness.

For example, perhaps there were moments when you engaged in actions that did not align with your values. You may have misused alcohol or substances as a coping mechanism for sensory and social challenges, or you may have fallen into other addiction to numb the pain. You may have hurt people you care about, or maybe you had some relationships end because you didn't yet know who you were and how to communicate your needs effectively. If you resorted to unhealthy strategies while striving to survive in a world not designed for you, know that you're not alone—you were doing the best you could with the resources and knowledge you had at the time.

Strive to release any blame, regret, and shame and redirect your focus toward embracing self-forgiveness and kindness, lightening the load on your mind and spirit.

# Grieve Your Limits
## *Autistic Mindset and Well-Being*

My autism diagnosis led me to feel liberation, pride—and also grief. The most profound moments of grief emerge when I come face-to-face with my own limits. These limits encompass sensory limits, energy limits, and social limits. If I ignore these limits, I'm making myself susceptible to burnout and chronic health conditions.

When I discovered I was Autistic, I changed career paths. I realized that working as a professor within an academic institute or working full-time in a hospital setting would utterly burn me out. There was grief in this realization, but on the other side of that grief was freedom. I restructured my life, built a company called Neurodivergent Insights, and embarked on a career that worked with my sensory, social, and energy limits. In order to find this happiness, I needed to both acknowledge and grieve my limits.

Grieving your limits is an ongoing process, not a one-time experience. Maybe one day you wake up and encounter a wall of fatigue, experience intensified executive functioning struggles, or strain to keep up with the demands of parenting. In these moments, it's perfectly fine to grieve your limits once again. However, on the other side of that grief is freedom: When you grieve your limits, you can actually construct realistic expectations and release yourself from the guilt of not conforming to the pace of your allistic peers. It's much better for your mental health to cultivate a pace and life that works for you and honors your limits!

# Celebrate Your Authenticity
# with an Identity Board
## *Autistic Mindset and Well-Being*

Autistic people often grapple with identity questions—especially those of us who have spent our lives masking our true selves. Masking can result in a diffuse sense of self, making it challenging to understand who you truly are. Engaging in activities that encourage self-reflection can be a powerful way to reclaim your identity. One fun and creative way to do that is to craft an "identity board," which is a visual and creative representation of your core values, interests, and identities.

To create an identity board, you have a few options:

- **Handcraft an identity board:** Gather images that reflect your core values, identities, and interests from magazines or online sources, then arrange them and glue them to a poster board. Add meaningful words, quotes, and symbols to create a visual representation of your authentic self.

- **Design a digital identity board:** Create a Pinterest or Canva board dedicated to your identity exploration. Search for images, quotes, and articles that align with your core values and reflect your interests. One advantage of a digital board is that it allows for even easier editing and updating as you continue to explore and develop your sense of self.

No matter which method you prefer, look for images that bring you joy and reflect your authentic self. When you're done for now, hang the board up where you can see and enjoy it regularly, or, if digital, make it readily accessible to pull up and visit. Let your board evolve alongside you, updating it every once in a while so that it can help fuel your journey of self-discovery, self-acceptance, and self-expression.

# Practice Gray Thinking
## *Mental Health Resilience*

All-or-nothing thinking—in which an event is either perceived as perfect or a complete failure—is common among Autistic people. During my early years as a mother, this mindset manifested as constant self-criticism about my parenting. Being Autistic, sleep-deprived, and raising two neurodivergent children, I wasn't always perfect (not even close!). However, due to all-or-nothing thinking, whenever I handled something imperfectly, I took that as evidence I was a terrible mother. Similarly, if I made a mistake in a friendship, I would distance myself, convinced that I was a wholly inadequate friend and had ruined the friendship.

This type of thinking can be detrimental to your mental health because it amplifies self-judgment and creates unrealistic expectations. It also sets you up for feelings of depression, low self-confidence, and disappointment. Whether it's one small setback in your day or a minor mishap in social situations, this kind of thinking tends to lead to inner criticism and a sense of failure.

The antidote to all-or-nothing thinking is practicing "gray thinking"—in other words, understanding that there *is* a middle ground and that mistakes and setbacks are a natural part of life. Catching instances of all-or-nothing thinking and then reframing them with more nuanced thoughts is a way of practicing gray thinking. For example, instead of labeling myself a terrible mother, I could acknowledge, "I am a good mother, and I didn't handle that situation like I wish I had."

And for some extra support, consider trying this simple yet effective linguistic trick to help get out of all-or-nothing thinking and toward more gray thinking. Pay attention to how you often use the word "but" to disqualify or negate something that's otherwise good. For instance, you might say, "The party was nice, but I made a fool of myself by being awkward." Notice how the second part of the sentence invalidates the positive aspect.

Instead, replace "but" with "and." For example, "The party was nice, *and* I had an awkward moment." Or "Today was a good day, *and* there were some challenging moments."

This small linguistic shift will help you challenge the binary thinking pattern and embrace a more nuanced perspective. It allows you to acknowledge positive and challenging aspects of your experiences, fostering a balanced and resilient mindset.

If you try to adopt a mindset of gray thinking, you can operate with more realistic expectations for yourself and acknowledge hardship without spiraling. This shift in perspective allows you to approach life's challenges with the compassion you deserve and the resilience inside you.

# Beware of Confirmation Bias
## *Mental Health Resilience*

Our minds are remarkable at scanning the world for evidence that supports our preexisting beliefs or hypotheses. This concept, known as confirmation bias, plays a significant role in shaping our perceptions of reality. Your brain naturally prioritizes information confirming your preconceived notions while downplaying or disregarding contradictory evidence. This shortcut helps your brain process information more efficiently so you can attempt to manage the vast amount of information you encounter daily. While it's a helpful shortcut, it can also cause distorted perceptions of reality.

This bias manifests in various aspects of our lives. For instance, people struggling with anxiety might selectively focus on evidence that confirms their anxious thoughts, while those who believe they are incompetent may fixate on instances in which they feel they made a mistake. Or if you believe someone doesn't like you, your mind will look for evidence of slights they've made toward you.

It's also crucial to acknowledge that the influence of confirmation bias extends beyond individual experiences and plays a role in shaping societal narratives. Confirmation bias can contribute to the perpetuation of harmful racial stereotypes and the formation of inaccurate beliefs about groups of people.

Awareness of confirmation bias is the first step in mitigating its influence. To counter these thoughts when they become apparent, first notice and name what filter you have on and then try seeking out diverse or alternative lenses or perspectives and engage in conversations that challenge your existing beliefs. This can help broaden your understanding and reduce the impact of confirmation bias on your decision-making.

# Expose the Stories
# Your Brain Is Telling You
## *Mental Health Resilience*

Our minds are master storytellers. As soon as we have experiences, our minds are off and running, telling wild stories related to the events. These stories unfold rapidly and automatically, often slipping under our radar. For example, after an awkward social interaction or a mistake on an assignment, your mind may spin stories like "I am socially awkward" or "I am incompetent."

Recognizing and "catching" the story that your mind is telling you at any given moment is a powerful practice. By becoming aware of the narrative playing in your mind, you gain the opportunity to expose it, unhook from it, and reclaim agency over your mind.

To do this, ask yourself: "What is the story my mind is currently weaving?" Just the act of acknowledging the story reduces its hold on you. Alternatively, you could try envisioning the narrative as a movie you're watching or a book you're reading. Contemplate, "What title would best encapsulate this cinematic or literary creation?" This exercise acknowledges the story's presence (thereby diminishing its influence) while also enabling you to perceive it as a distinct entity rather than an unquestionable reality.

Thinking of your thoughts as stories can help you detach from their grip and allow you to create more empowering narratives that align with your true self.

# Change Your Relationship to Your Thoughts

## *Mental Health Resilience*

Your thoughts have a profound impact on your mental well-being. While certain therapies, such as cognitive behavioral therapy (CBT), emphasize changing your thoughts, many Autistic people find that engaging in these techniques can have adverse effects. It can feel invalidating or dismissive of our experiences of marginalization. Or it can lead to a rebound effect, where we become more entrenched in a wrestling match with our thoughts, resulting in heightened internal debates and increased distress.

Due to the unique ability many Autistic people have to perceive things from multiple angles, changing your thoughts may not always be effective. In my personal experience, and from what I've observed in many Autistic people, we tend to have better luck when we *change our relationship to our thoughts versus changing our thoughts themselves.* By changing your relationship with your thoughts, you can cultivate a healthier and more balanced connection with them.

As discussed in the Expose the Stories Your Brain Is Telling You entry in this chapter, one way to deal with this is to remember that you don't have to believe every thought that comes into your mind. Instead, try thinking of your mind as a third party that's coming up with these ideas.

For instance, when I notice negative self-talk, I might say, "*My mind* is telling me I'm not good right now." Similarly, in therapy sessions, I might reflect to a client, "So *your mind* is going on about how bad you are right now." By treating your mind as if it were another entity, you gain a sense of distance. This practice allows you to observe the mind's thoughts without automatically accepting them as facts or absolute truths.

Another technique to unhook from your thoughts is cognitive defusion. It involves recognizing that thoughts are mental events and not objective truths. By envisioning thoughts as passing clouds in the sky or trains swiftly moving by, you can practice allowing them to come and go without becoming entangled in their content. This metaphorical perspective helps cultivate a sense of detachment as you observe your thoughts from a distance without feeling compelled to act upon or believe every single one.

For a brief self-check, courtesy of my colleague Wes Gos, an Autistic therapist hailing from Canada, ask yourself: "Are you having the thought or is the thought having you?" If you discover that the thought is the one orchestrating the show, it's time to create some distance from it and see if you can unhook!

Practicing self-compassion is another powerful way to unhook from painful thoughts. You might consider offering gentleness instead of harshly judging yourself or getting caught in self-criticism. Normalizing the experience of intrusive or unhelpful thoughts can reduce their impact. Rather than engaging in a fight with the accuracy of the thought, you can instead simply acknowledge it as a painful thought you are experiencing.

The goal is not to eliminate all negative or distressing thoughts—that's unrealistic—but rather to relate to them in a healthier and more balanced way. By changing your relationship to your thoughts, you can cultivate greater mental flexibility and a sense of inner spaciousness and freedom.

# Identify Cognitive Distortions
## *Mental Health Resilience*

Our minds are remarkably sneaky and deceptive, employing filters known as cognitive distortions. These filters can subtly influence our mental well-being, often leading to negative thoughts and self-judgment.

To understand cognitive distortions, think of them as akin to wearing blue-tinted sunglasses that color everything you see. Just as the blue tint distorts your visual perception, cognitive distortions skew your understanding of reality, reinforce negative beliefs, and contribute to emotional suffering.

Becoming aware of these distortions allows you to distance yourself and release from their grip. Rather than trying to argue your way out of them, you may benefit more from learning to unhook from these distortions—as I have found to be the case with Autistic people I have worked with.

Here are some common cognitive distortions to be mindful of:

- **All-or-nothing thinking:** This involves perceiving situations in extreme terms of either success or failure without considering the gray areas in between. It can limit your ability to see nuance, hinder problem-solving, and lead to overly negative thinking. See more on this topic in the Practice Gray Thinking entry in this chapter.

- **Overgeneralization:** This involves drawing broad conclusions based on limited evidence or a single negative experience. It can perpetuate negative beliefs, contribute to self-doubt, and create a narrow and biased perception of yourself and the world.

- **Jumping to conclusions:** This occurs when you make negative assumptions or interpretations without sufficient evidence. It can fuel anxiety, strain relationships, and lead to misunderstandings as you rush to judgment without considering alternative explanations or gathering enough information.

- **Emotional reasoning:** This involves basing the truth or validity of a thought on your emotions rather than on objective evidence. For example, if you feel anxious about giving a presentation and think, "I feel so anxious, so I must be terrible at public speaking," you're engaging in emotional reasoning. This cognitive distortion can intensify emotional distress as your feelings dictate your thoughts and decisions.

- **Mind reading:** This occurs when you assume, without concrete evidence, that you know what others are thinking or how they perceive you. It can undermine your self-confidence, create social anxiety, and lead to misinterpretations and misunderstandings in your interactions with others.

- **Future telling:** Future telling involves making predictions and assumptions about future events, often based on limited information or personal biases. This can lead to excessive worry, anxiety, and an unrealistic focus on worst-case scenarios.

Consider which distortions your mind is prone to. The next time you notice your mind filtering your reality through these lenses, pause and mindfully name what is happening. For example, say, "Right now, my mind is engaging in mind reading about what others think of me." Identifying the cognitive distortion in action helps you unhook from the painful thoughts and scripts, loosening their grip in the moment and empowering you to reclaim agency over your own thinking. Keep in mind the goal is not to eliminate these thoughts entirely—that's not realistic—but rather to reduce their grasp on you in the present moment, enhance your sense of agency, and improve your mental health (remember, try and have the thought versus letting the thought have you!).

# Get Unhooked: Eight Ways to Unhook from Painful Thoughts

## *Mental Health Resilience*

Unhooking or defusing from painful thoughts is a skill commonly taught in acceptance and commitment therapy (ACT). This practice can be very helpful if you're prone to anxious thoughts, negative self-talk, rumination, or the frequent intrusion of cognitive distortions into your mind!

Here are some strategies to help you break free from distressing and painful thoughts:

- **Thought labeling:** Practice thought labeling by saying, "I am noticing I am having the thought that…" before your distressing thought. This simple act helps you create distance from the thought and see it for what it is—a painful thought your mind is "gifting" you.

- **Silly songs:** Put your painful thoughts to a silly song, like the birthday song or a nursery rhyme. Sing the thought out loud with playful tunes to lessen its grip.

- **Cloud visualization:** Imagine your distressing thought as a cloud passing by in the sky. Watch it drift away without holding on to it. Recognize that thoughts, like clouds, come and go. You can also use alternative imagery such as a passing train, a car driving by, or a leaf floating down a stream.

- **Mindful observation:** Engage in mindful observation by describing the details of your distressing thought. Observe it as you would a painting, noticing its colors, shapes, and patterns.

- **Thanking your mind:** Thank your mind for generating the thought, recognizing that it's trying to protect you. Then gently let it know that you've got things covered for now.

- **Breathing and releasing:** As you breathe in, acknowledge your painful thought. As you breathe out, imagine releasing it with your exhale. This practice helps you let go of the thought's hold on you.

- **Thought sculpting:** Treat your thought as a sculptor would clay. Mold it into amusing shapes or characters to make it less intimidating.

- **A gratitude ritual:** Practice a short gratitude ritual by naming three things you're grateful for whenever a distressing thought arises. This practice redirects your attention toward positivity (our brains have a hard time redirecting attention when hooked, and the gratitude ritual helps with this!).

You can employ these techniques whenever you become aware of a cognitive distortion, distressing narrative, or challenging thought. By disengaging from these painful thoughts, you regain a sense of control, enabling you to decide how you wish to address and manage them. This process also frees up valuable mental space, allowing you to reclaim your precious mental real estate to invest it in the things you value and care about!

# Practice Mindfulness on the Go
## *Mental Health Resilience*

We know that mindfulness is good for mental health. You've likely heard this hundreds of times! However, mindfulness can be challenging for neurodivergent people (especially those of us whose autism comes with a side of ADHD).

Sitting down and attempting to do a traditional mindfulness exercise is frustrating and exhausting for me. It isn't active enough, so my mind naturally diverges a hundred ways! For this reason, I prefer mindfulness-on-the-go activities, and you might as well.

Try to think of mindfulness as a way of being with yourself more so than a quiet, still activity. Whenever you observe your thoughts without judgment or evaluation, you are being mindful. You can do this wherever you are, and you don't need to engage in a traditional mindfulness exercise like meditation to relate to yourself in this way! One helpful way to conceptualize mindfulness is to think of your mind in two parts: the part that's observing things and the part that's evaluating them.

In daily life, we often operate from the evaluative part of our minds, where we constantly assess and judge our experiences. Consider a scenario where you're giving a presentation. As you speak, thoughts flood your mind, evaluating your performance: "Am I speaking clearly enough? Did I miss any important points? Are people engaged?" These evaluative thoughts arise almost automatically, shaping your perception of the situation and influencing your emotions—and they're not an example of being mindful.

Your observing brain, on the other hand, acts as a detached observer and narrator. When you're observing, you simply witness and acknowledge the present moment without judgment. For example, you might think, "This is a challenging moment right now" or "I feel stressed about that interaction" as you observe and narrate your experience. Embracing you observing mind enables you to cultivate nonjudgmental awareness and practice mindfulness wherever you are.

Here are some mindfulness-on-the-go activities that you can incorporate into your daily life:

- **Identify the script:** Become aware of the recurring thoughts or patterns that arise in your mind. Notice the narratives or stories that play out, and recognize them as mental scripts.

- **Name the thought:** Practice labeling your thoughts with a simple observation, such as "I am noticing I am having the thought ____." For example, if the thought "I'm not good enough" arises, you might say, "I am noticing I am having the thought 'I'm not good enough.'" This naming process brings your observing mind online, which helps create distance from the thought and allows you to gain a mindful perspective into your current experience.

- **Separate yourself a bit from your mind:** Engage in a conversation with your mind, treating it as a separate entity, and don't be afraid to add a touch of sass as you interact with it!

Mindfulness does not always have to be about maintaining a fixed state of focus. Instead, just relate to your thoughts with openness, nonjudgment, and curiosity.

# Expand Your "Window of Tolerance"
## Mental Health Resilience

The "window of tolerance" is a concept that represents your body's capacity to handle and respond to various levels of stress. When you are within your window of tolerance, you are in a balanced state, able to think clearly, engage with others, and handle everyday stressors effectively.

When you exceed the upper threshold of your window, you may enter a *hyper*aroused state characterized by anxiety, agitation, and panic. On the other hand, if you drop below the threshold, you may enter a *hypo*aroused state marked by dissociation, fatigue, numbness, and a sense of detachment.

Neurodivergent people tend to have a narrower window of tolerance, meaning we more easily flip into a stressed state. However, the good news is you can teach it how to expand, allowing you to handle a broader range of emotional and sensory experiences. By actively working on expanding your window of tolerance, you can enhance resilience and navigate challenging situations with greater ease, since you're responding from a place of balance and inner harmony.

Here are some ways to cultivate a wider window of tolerance:

- **Practice self-regulation:** Self-regulation skills help you recognize and manage your emotions effectively. Grounding techniques and relaxation strategies can help you regulate your nervous system during challenging situations.

- **Prioritize self-care:** Make sure to practice self-care that nourishes your mind and body, which helps support a resilient nervous system.

- **Set boundaries:** Establish and maintain healthy boundaries in your relationships and daily life. Learn to say no when necessary and prioritize your needs to avoid becoming overwhelmed.

- **Go to therapy:** Seek professional support from a therapist who specializes in trauma or stress management. Therapy can provide valuable tools and strategies to process difficult emotions, heal past wounds, and expand your window of tolerance.

- **Map your nervous system:** You can explore nervous system mapping on your own or with the guidance of a therapist or coach. This process involves identifying and tracking your nervous system states, helping you gain a deeper understanding of your current state and enabling better self-regulation.

- **Prioritize gut health:** Nourishing your gut through a balanced diet, probiotics, and mindful eating practices can support a healthier nervous system and contribute to a wider window of tolerance. (See Support Your Gut Health in Chapter 2 for more information.)

- **Increase vagal tone:** Engage in practices that increase vagal tone (see Stimulate Your Vagus Nerve for Stress Relief in Chapter 2). Stimulation of the vagus nerve can reduce stress.

- **Get biofeedback:** Enhance self-regulation skills and expand your capacity to tolerate challenging emotions and situations through biofeedback training. Biofeedback involves gaining awareness of your physiological responses, such as heart rate, skin temperature, and muscle tension, and learning techniques to influence these responses. To get started with biofeedback, you can seek out qualified practitioners or use home biofeedback devices and apps that are designed to help you develop these skills.

Expanding your window of tolerance is a gradual process that requires patience and persistence, but it's worth the effort. As you expand your window of tolerance, you'll find yourself better equipped to navigate life's challenges with greater ease.

# CHAPTER FIVE

• • •

# Social Self-Care

A few years ago, I wrote, "My soul longs for connection, and my body craves isolation." On the one hand, I crave connection, community, and belonging. On the other hand, being in a room with another human body overwhelms me. Not to mention the challenges of navigating social differences, group dynamics, and cross-neurotype interactions! You might recognize some of these feelings too.

From sensory limitations to cultural and communication differences to being misunderstood by those around us, Autistic people encounter numerous barriers when it comes to establishing social connections and a sense of belonging. But social connectedness is incredibly important for overall health, both physically and mentally! Discovering how to authentically connect with people while staying true to yourself is a powerful act of self-care.

When it comes to social self-care, there are two distinct aspects to consider: first, how to navigate an allistic world with minimal harm to yourself, and second, how to forge authentic and meaningful relationships. These objectives are slightly different because the strategies that help you survive in an allistic world may assist you in securing a job or accessing education, but they might not be the right strategies for fostering a genuine sense of connection with others. This chapter will address both of these social goals.

Topics are broken down into the categories of authentic relationships, interactions with neurotypicals, healthy relationships, and romantic relationships. Entries focus on a range of topics, such as navigating conflicting sensory needs, embracing Autistic communication styles, strategic use of self-disclosure, and more. You have so much to offer those around you— building strong relationships can foster meaningful connections that help you feel seen and provide a sense of belonging.

# Make Connections
# Through Special Interests
## *Authentic Relationships*

While allistic people often establish relationships through small talk and social-based conversations, Autistic people usually feel the strongest sense of connection when engaging with others over shared interests and values. Part of taking care of yourself is becoming aware of these preferences so you can create social experiences that work for you.

Your interests and values are deeply integrated into your identity and sense of self. When you delve into the intricacies of a special interest, you open up and share your inner world with another person. Precisely because your values and interests are closely intertwined with your identity, you'll likely feel most connected with others when relating over shared values and interests.

Here are some ways to forge friendships around your interests:

- Identify your special interests: Start by discovering your passions and interests, as these will be your common ground with potential friends.

- Join relevant communities: Seek out groups, clubs, or online forums that align with your interests and values.

- Engage actively: Participate in discussions and activities within your chosen communities, sharing your thoughts and experiences.

- Be patient: Building authentic friendships takes time, so allow connections to develop naturally, and practice patience.

By embracing the power of connecting through shared interests and ideals, you create opportunities to engage authentically with others. These connections can be rich and fulfilling, allowing you to foster authentic relationships based on shared passions and values.

# Understand the
# Double Empathy Problem
## *Authentic Relationships*

Have you ever experienced a disconnection between yourself and the people around you? Building authentic relationships can be challenging, particularly when you're striving to bridge the invisible gap with non-Autistic people!

Unfortunately, prevailing autism narratives often blame failed social encounters on the Autistic person's "deficits." People figuratively point fingers at Autistic people, accusing us of a lack of empathy and an inability to understand the perspectives of others (the ability to think about other people's mental states is often referred to as "theory of mind"). These assumptions fail to consider that non-Autistic people *also* experience empathy and theory of mind challenges when communicating across different neurotypes.

The "double empathy problem" offers a fresh perspective that challenges this prevailing view. Dr. Damian Milton, an Autistic sociologist, introduced this concept in the journal *Disability & Society* in 2012 to shed light on the mutual difficulties both parties face in understanding each other's frames of reference. It invites people to recognize that the difficulties and misunderstandings they encounter in social interactions emerge from a shared struggle to understand one another.

It acknowledges that when people with different neurotypes interact, a breakdown in communication occurs in both directions. This breakdown arises not from any inherent deficits in Autistic individuals but rather from the differences in communication styles each person is bringing to the table. It is through these differences that the breakdown emerges, and the wider the gap in neurocognitive styles, the more pronounced the communication challenges.

Supporting Milton's hypothesis, empirical studies (such as one published in 2020 by *Frontiers in Psychology*) have shown the impact of neurotype on social interactions. These studies paired participants based on their neurotype and revealed that Autistic people were able to build rapport effectively with one another, as were non-Autistic individuals. However, the most challenging pairings were between Autistic and non-Autistic individuals. Additional research has shown that Autistic people experience heightened closeness, rapport, reciprocity, and comfort in disclosing personal information when they're with fellow Autistic people. And it makes sense that Autistic people find it easier to establish connections with others who share our neurotype!

The key point to remember with the double empathy problem is that you possess a distinct social interaction style and culture, not a deficit in social skills.

Social-communication difficulties occur in the space between two different styles and are not due to one person only. Try to reject those simplistic narratives that place the blame on the Autistic person and instead consider this challenge through a broader cross-cultural lens.

We can build stronger social bonds if everyone collectively assumes responsibility for understanding and embracing one another. By valuing a diversity of communication styles, we can forge deeper connections, cultivate empathy, and celebrate the beauty of neurodiversity.

# Embrace High-Context Communication
## Authentic Relationships

Autistic people have a distinct communication style. One component of that is context-heavy communication. Context-heavy communication can look like giving a lot of background.

When sharing an idea, I feel compelled to provide the complete context. For instance, during a recent podcast episode, I shared a simple example of how understanding my neurodivergence has improved communication with my spouse. However, I found myself unpacking the entire backstory of how my spouse and I got to this conversation! Every idea I have exists in a specific context. Context permeates every aspect of my thoughts. This model might resonate with you too.

And it's not just that we communicate in a context-heavy way; we also need context to understand as listeners. This may involve asking numerous questions. Many of us construct mental context maps to provide frameworks for anchoring the information. You may notice that you need more context than an allistic speaker is providing. That's perfectly fine! Your brain is seeking context to facilitate understanding and retention of ideas.

Some discomfort can arise because Autistic people are often chastised for "providing too much detail." While it is good to be mindful that not everyone may have the patience for your context-heavy communication style, you should not feel ashamed of it.

Here are some ways to embrace high-context communication:

- If you have difficulty knowing what context questions to ask, consider preparing ahead of time. Think about the most critical pieces of context you need in order to navigate a particular conversation.

- When responding to contextless queries, having a few key phrases on hand can be helpful for those moments when you feel confused. For example, you can respond with, "That question is kind of vague; can you provide me more context for why you are asking?" Or, when someone poses a broad question like, "Tell me about yourself," you might respond with, "That's a broad question; what specifically would you like to know?"

- It's also helpful to recognize that not everyone may have the patience for the level of detail you naturally provide (or ask for). One approach is to follow up later or over email with additional questions, allowing you to delve into the specifics when the timing is right. You may even ask the person, "Would it be better if I followed up over email with additional questions?" This way, if the person is in the middle of a transition or occupied, they can address your questions at a more convenient time.

Your brain naturally associates ideas with their respective contexts, adding richness to your thought processes, and while this may not always be appreciated by those around you, remember this is part of the richness that adds to the deep processing style of Autistic brains.

# Connect with Others
# Through Story Swapping
## *Authentic Relationships*

Have you ever heard a friend share something that happened to them, then instinctively responded by sharing a similar experience you had? That's called story swapping, and it tends to be a natural communication method for Autistic people. Within Autistic culture, story swapping serves as a means of connecting, relating, and expressing empathy. However, this tendency is unfortunately often misunderstood by allistic culture as redirecting the focus onto ourselves instead of genuinely aiming to connect.

When you are among fellow Autistic people, you will likely find that connecting through shared story swapping is a natural and comfortable way to bond. Finding opportunities to story swap is a great way to create and strengthen social connections.

If you would like to make your story swapping more allistic friendly when interacting with allistic people, here's a helpful strategy to consider: Try doing what I call the "dance back": After sharing your own story, make a conscious effort to redirect the attention back to them (you're "dancing" the conversation back to them). For example, after sharing a relatable story, you might say, "When that happened to me, I felt really vulnerable. Was it intense for you as well?" Alternatively, if you're discussing a challenging work situation, you can smoothly transition by saying, "I experienced something similar at work (insert your story here). It was quite stressful, and I remember feeling overwhelmed. How did you handle the stress?" By explicitly linking your experience to theirs, you demonstrate a genuine interest in their perspective and an empathetic desire to connect and learn more.

It is also always beneficial to approach conversations with curiosity rather than assuming how the other person feels, as most people respond more positively to curiosity. The "dance back" approach allows you to honor your natural story-swapping instinct while deepening your interactions.

# Play in Parallel
## *Authentic Relationships*

Sometimes, I jokingly say that one of the reasons I married my spouse is because our early dates revolved around coffee shops, books, and writing. We excelled at parallel play. Parallel play (or parallel work) refers to engaging in a solo activity alongside someone else doing a similar solo activity. For Autistic people, parallel play allows each person to engage in their own activities while still enjoying the presence and connection of another person.

Whether it's reading in the same room as a partner, friend, or family member; studying alongside a classmate; or spending time immersed in your interest while someone else does the same nearby, parallel play can help you form social connections in a way that works for you and your body.

To give this a try, you can start by asking a friend to join you in playing video games, visiting a coffee shop to read, or studying. If meeting in person isn't feasible, you can also explore virtual options. For example, you can set up a Zoom call and work on a project simultaneously, creating a virtual workspace.

See if you both appreciate the comfort and closeness that come from sharing space and time together, even when pursuing your individual interests.

# Join in Autistic Culture
## *Authentic Relationships*

In recent years, there has been a notable increase in Autistic spaces specifically created by and for Autistic people. A 2019 article in *Metaphilosophy* described accounts of many Autistic people having an immediate sense of belonging and feeling at home when stepping into these spaces. Interestingly, when allistic people enter these spaces, they often express feelings of anxiety, self-doubt, and confusion about how to interact with others. These observations reflect the existence of a distinct Autistic culture.

But what exactly is Autistic culture? Autistic culture encompasses the shared experiences, perspectives, values, and ways of being that are unique to the Autistic community. It goes beyond individual traits and describes a collective culture formed by the lived experiences of Autistic people.

Connecting with Autistic culture, whether through physical spaces, online platforms, or digital communities, is a powerful self-care practice that allows you to build bonds while being yourself. It is through these relationships that many of us finally experience a sense of belonging, connectedness, and authentic engagement. Discovering Autistic spaces and culture can empower you to have the courage to unmask and explore your true self.

Here are a few ways you can engage with Autistic culture as a way to build meaningful social connections to the community at large:

- **Seek out Autistic-led communities:** Look for online communities, forums, and social media groups that are led by and centered around Autistic voices. These spaces allow you to interact with people with similar experiences and perspectives.

- **Participate in Autistic events and gatherings:** Attend conferences, workshops, neurodivergent affinity groups, and meetups specifically organized by and for Autistic people. These events provide opportunities to connect with others, learn from their insights, and engage in discussions about topics relevant to the Autistic community. (Note: Neurodivergent groups are becoming more prevalent in workplaces and educational institutions, so be sure to check if your school or workplace offers these opportunities!)

- **Explore Autistic arts, literature, and media:** Dive into the rich world of Autistic creativity and expression. Discover Autistic authors, artists, filmmakers, and musicians whose works reflect the diverse experiences and talents within the Autistic community. Engaging with their creations can deepen your understanding of and connection to Autistic culture.

- **Educate yourself about Autistic history and activism:** Learn about the history of the Autistic rights movement, advocacy efforts, and achievements of Autistic activists. Familiarize yourself with the challenges faced by the Autistic community and the progress made in promoting acceptance, inclusion, and neurodiversity.

- **Engage in dialogue and listen to Autistic voices:** Actively seek out Autistic perspectives by reading blogs, articles, and books written by Autistic authors. Listen to Autistic podcasts to hear about lived experiences. Consider following Autistic activists, advocates, and influencers on social media to gain insights and stay updated on important conversations within the Autistic community.

The Autistic community is a rich place where you can make connections you didn't even realize existed. Try reaching out in ways you feel comfortable with—you'll likely have interesting experiences and find meaningful connections.

# Embrace Object-Based Conversations
## *Authentic Relationships*

Dr. Marilyn Monteiro is a clinician, writer, and researcher and the founder of the MIGDAS, one of the few affirming autism assessments available. I had a light bulb moment while listening to her training on how she assesses Autistic children. She emphasized the value of leading with object-based conversations rather than social-based conversations when first meeting Autistic children. Social-based conversations, starting with questions like "How are you?" or "Tell me about yourself," often cause Autistic children to freeze and retreat inward. However, when you begin a conversation by delving into a specific topic, particularly one of interest to the child, you witness them open up and engage more readily.

This understanding of object-based versus social-based conversation helped me make sense of thirty-seven years of communication struggles. I had often wondered why I found questions like "Tell me about yourself" or "What did you do this weekend?" challenging, while I could effortlessly dive into discussions about books, ideas, philosophy, and psychology. It was because social-based questions often trigger a mini freeze response in many Autistic people. These questions tend to be vague and abstract, and it is challenging to succinctly capture the intricacies of our inner worlds in a single answer. Plus, they can also feel intrusive, acting as a sensory demand that requires us to quickly process and respond.

Thinking of these conversation styles using a visual might help you understand them even more thoroughly. For social-based conversations, imagine two individuals facing each other, engaging in a dialogue centered around themselves. For object-based conversations, picture a scene where two people stand side by side, their attention directed toward a captivating sunset as they discuss the intricacies of its beauty. If you find object-based conversations more enjoyable for you, embrace them! Recognizing and accepting your preferred communication styles is a really effective way to take care of your social self and built authentic connections.

To embrace object-based conversations in your life, consider coming up with conversation starters that are focused on objects or topics rather than purely social elements. This proactive shift can create opportunities for engaging discussions.

Here are a few examples that work in a wide variety of settings:

- "Tell me about an interesting idea you've learned recently."
- "Have you read any good books lately?"
- "What's a fascinating news story that has caught your attention recently?"
- "Do you have a particular hobby or activity that you enjoy?"

You will likely still find yourself in social-based conversations, however. When that happens, you can learn to pivot the conversation back to object-based topics while still addressing the initial inquiry. For instance, if someone says, "Tell me about yourself," you can respond by saying, "That's quite a broad question, but let me share some things I am passionate about and spend a lot of time learning about." By shifting the conversation to more concrete and object-based spaces, you can stay comfortable and true to yourself while still engaging with the person.

# Decide Whether to
# Tell People You Are Autistic
## Interactions with Neurotypicals

Telling other people that you are Autistic can be a daunting and anxiety-inducing journey, especially when navigating interactions with neurotypicals. The delicate dance of revealing your true self while grappling with the fear of judgment and misconceptions can make the process both challenging and emotionally charged.

Unfortunately, we live in a world that still heavily stigmatizes autism. This means that when you choose to disclose that you are Autistic, there are some potential negative outcomes to consider. First, the person may misperceive you and make assumptions about you based on their limited understanding. Second, you may find yourself in the position of needing to educate them about autism, which can create awkwardness and tension within the relationship.

When it comes to self-disclosure, it's important to remember that it doesn't have to be an all-or-nothing approach. Partial self-disclosure allows you to gauge the person's response and make further decisions based on that.

Examples of partial self-disclosure include statements such as:

- "I am neurodivergent."
- "I sometimes need extra time to process information."
- "I may not always make eye contact."
- "I struggle with unexpected changes in plans."

If the person responds to a statement like this positively, showing understanding, you may feel more comfortable disclosing more about yourself. However, if their response is judgmental or not supportive, it may be safer to maintain some privacy about your identity in that particular relationship.

Another advantage of not sharing everything up front is that it allows the disclosure to match the pace of closeness in the relationship. What you choose to share on a first meeting or date may differ from what you disclose on a fifth, as trust and closeness develop over time.

Alternatively, some people may opt for complete openness about their Autistic identity, as they want to interact only with those who are already Autistic affirming. This is also a valid choice. (This is why I have chosen to be an openly Autistic psychologist—it helps me connect with Autistic clients and professionals.) However, not everyone has the privilege or safety of being openly Autistic. In these cases, it can be helpful to have prepreared partial self-disclosure statements ready, allowing you to navigate conversations thoughtfully and protect your well-being.

It's also important to prioritize your own well-being when navigating self-disclosure. Recognize that you alone have the right to set boundaries and choose what you disclose about your neurodivergent identity. Self-disclosure is a personal decision based on your comfort level and the trust you have established with the other person. Building authentic relationships requires mutual respect and acceptance, and deciding what you share, when, how, and with whom is your choice to make. Surrounding yourself with understanding and accepting people who respect and value you for who you are is a powerful act of social self-care.

# Craft Scripts for Boundary-Setting and Transitions
## Interactions with Neurotypicals

Navigating small talk and surface-level interactions can be exhausting and challenging for many Autistic people. Preprepared scripts work as a helpful tool for navigating these situations and reducing anxiety. Scripts are brief statements or blurbs you come up with and rehearse before engaging in social interactions, allowing you to feel more prepared and confident in social situations.

Many Autistic people intuitively engage in this practice. For years I spent a copious amount of time having pretend conversations. Only after my diagnosis did I realize what I was doing—I was developing social scripts and practicing so that I wouldn't feel so caught off guard during social moments.

Some scripting can be seen as a form of masking, since it involves pre-planning and rehearsing statements. While I am not advocating for masking as a general practice, this particular exercise can help reduce anxiety and promote self-advocacy skills. In specific scenarios, using preprepared scripts can be beneficial, particularly when they resonate with your authentic self and act as tools for self-advocacy. This approach transforms them into tools for self-empowerment rather than tools for masking your identity.

Let's explore some scenarios where utilizing social scripts can be helpful:

- **Boundary-setting:** Setting boundaries can be challenging, especially for Autistic people. Learning and practicing simple phrases like "No, I'm sorry, I am not able to do that right now" or "I'm not comfortable answering that question" can provide you with ready-made responses for high-pressure moments when formulating boundary statements on the spot may be difficult.

- **Small talk/introductions:** Small talk can often be anxiety inducing for many of us. It's helpful to have a few statements ready to quickly answer questions, transition the conversation, or politely exit. For example, having an exit statement ready can help you gracefully leave the conversation with more ease by saying, "It's been lovely chatting with you" or "It was a pleasure to meet you." These phrases can help you navigate these moments with greater ease, making social interactions more comfortable.

- **Self-advocacy:** There are moments when advocating for yourself becomes essential, especially in high-stress situations. During such times, it can be challenging to gather your thoughts and express your needs effectively. It's helpful to have preprepared self-advocacy statements at your disposal. For instance, you can say something like, "I'm finding this situation very stressful, and I need a moment to collect my thoughts. Can we pause for a few minutes, or can you give me some space to regroup?" These prepared statements empower you to communicate your needs clearly and assertively, ensuring that your concerns are addressed effectively.

To make the most of social scripts, write them down and practice saying them aloud, or engage in rehearsing conversations when alone. The goal is to become comfortable with the words so that, in high-pressure moments, there is a sense of muscle memory that allows you to say the words more easily.

Brainstorming social scripts ahead of time can reduce anxiety and support your social self-care. Used properly, they can provide a sense of empowerment and confidence, allowing you to communicate your authentic self to others more effectively.

# Practice Context Awareness
## Interactions with Neurotypicals

Context adjustment, the process of adapting to varying social norms and behaviors in different situations and settings, can be challenging for Autistic people. While this difficulty is also commonly known as "context blindness," I find the term coined by Autistic psychologist Dr. Amara Brook, "context independence," more fitting. Context independence means your behavior lives and exists independent of your context. Given this, you may struggle to understand how social rules apply in one context but not another. For instance, why is it acceptable to ask certain questions at a social gathering but not in a work context? Why is a certain pickup line appropriate in a bar but not in the grocery store? Allistic brains pick up these context cues sub-cortically, meaning that their brains intuitively sense them without having to analytically decode all the rules and norms!

While I recognize the challenges of not intuitively picking up context cues, I don't embrace the term "context blindness." Instead of defining this experience by our deficits, I prefer focusing on what we excel at—I see it as a reflection of our profound appreciation for authenticity and our ability to stay true to ourselves, hence why I prefer the term "context independence."

We tend to maintain our authenticity when interacting with people from all walks of life, whether it's a janitor or a CEO. Given the high value we place on authenticity, we often find altering our behavior, actions, and words for various contexts to be inauthentic.

However, because society operates based on an unwritten rule book, context independence can lead to misunderstandings. For instance, Autistic people, particularly cis-het (cisgender-heterosexual) men, disproportionally face accusations of sexual harassment or stalking due to behaviors caused by difficulties understanding context cues around romantic advancements (for example, asking a girl out multiple times or intentionally hanging out where he knows she will be in order to initiate conversation). This confusion is especially perilous for Black and Brown Autistic men, as grasping these contextual rules can become a matter of safety.

Understanding context cues can help prevent you from getting fired and being accused of sexual harassment and even crimes.

Here are some strategies to navigate the hidden rule book:

- **Seek guidance from friends:** Ask non-Autistic friends and family to help decode the implicit rules. Request their feedback on specific situations.

- **Reflect on experiences:** Take time to reflect on any negative experiences and consider where the interactions went awry. Were there hidden rules or expectations you were unaware of but now know? Writing down your reflections can help you develop "social templates" to understand expected interactions in different social environments.

- **Request explicit feedback and rules from employers:** It can be particularly confusing to figure out the protocol in workplaces, where socializing and professionalism are mixed. Ask your employers for explicit feedback and clarification on social expectations.

While the authenticity you bring to the world is something to celebrate, it can also leave you vulnerable. For this reason, developing some context-shifting skills can be an important way to protect yourself when interacting with allistic people. It's not about completely conforming or shapeshifting, changing who you are, but rather finding a balance that respects both your authenticity and the invisible societal rules around you.

# Navigate Conflict
## Interactions with Neurotypicals

Conflict is difficult for all humans, but it's especially challenging when it involves individuals with different neurotypes.

Here are two insights gleaned from the school of hard knocks and the mishaps of my own experience:

- Consider other people's emotions: As someone who tends to approach conflicts with a factual mindset, I used to believe that if I could just present the facts, both parties would understand each other and resolve the disagreement. However, I've come to realize that many allistic people operate more from their emotions during conflict. Offering emotional validation such as "That sounds really painful" or "It makes sense you would feel that way" goes a long way in de-escalating conflict.

- Sometimes less is more: During conflicts, I tend to overexplain and provide excessive context, believing that if the other person grasped the full context and relational dynamics, we could effectively work through the issue. However, my sister once offered me valuable insight: "When you provide extra details, it can come across as defensiveness. Sometimes less is more." I hadn't realized that my strong desire to be understood was perceived as defensiveness. This feedback has proven invaluable. Although it can be challenging to implement, I have found it to be quite helpful in de-escalating conflicts.

Managing conflicts isn't necessarily a fun part of self-care, but it's worth the time and effort to try to make disagreements more civil and productive.

# Identify Red Flags and Green Flags in Friendship

## Healthy Relationships

Autistic people are more vulnerable to being taken advantage of because we have more difficulty reading social cues and recognizing deceptive behavior. That's why it's a useful social self-care practice to reflect on red and green flags in friendships and relationships—in other words, positive and negative signs that can help you assess the health of the friendship.

Here are prompts to help you think about what you want in a friendship:

- What qualities or actions make you feel respected in a friendship?
- What communication styles or actions contribute to effective listening from a friend?
- What level of reliability and responsiveness do you expect from a friend?
- What types of support and encouragement do you value in a friendship?
- How do you want your neurodivergent traits to be respected and valued in a friendship?
- How do you prefer conflicts or disagreements to be addressed?
- What are your expectations regarding privacy and confidentiality?

As you answer these questions, pay attention to your instincts to identify your personal green flags (qualities that show that the relationship is meeting your needs) and red flags (concerning behaviors that don't align with your preferences). Fulfilling friendships are an important part of your social life, and knowing what works for you and what doesn't will help you surround yourself with friends who love and respect you just as you are.

# Deal with Rejection Sensitivity
## *Healthy Relationships*

"Rejection sensitivity" is a term that describes a heightened sensitivity and intense emotional reaction to perceived rejection—and it's common among ADHDers and Autistic people. Rejection sensitivity makes a lot of sense from a social-evolution perspective. In ancient times, belonging to a group was crucial for a person's safety. Being excluded or ostracized posed significant threats to survival, making belonging synonymous with survival itself!

Even though life is different today, belonging to a social group is still a vital part of being human. As Autistic people, we often feel like outsiders, frequently experiencing threats to our sense of belonging. Consequently, our fight-or-flight responses can be triggered as if our very survival is at stake. Despite the modern understanding that it is not a life-or-death situation, our bodies continue to react as if it were.

Rejection sensitivity plays several tricks on your brain. When you are used to feeling rejection, your mind becomes more attuned to it. And because Autistic people *do* experience more rejection, our brains are typically primed to see it! This unconscious scanning for signs of rejection can result in "false alarms," where we perceive rejection even when it is not actually present. The slightest look, tone of voice, or comment can trigger feelings of rejection. When that happens, we can miss out on connecting with a new friend or deepening an existing friendship.

Becoming aware of this phenomenon will help you minimize its impacts on your relationships. Then you can move on to acknowledging when rejection sensitivity is at play, saying to yourself, "That's my rejection sensitivity acting up." Statements like this create some distance from the immediate emotional reaction and allow you to detach from it. Finally, think about those early humans, and accept the ingrained biological forces at play. This practice can also help alleviate feelings of shame about your rejection sensitivity, because you can place it within the larger tapestry of human history.

# Balance Social Connection and Alone Time

## *Healthy Relationships*

Before I discovered I was Autistic, I had a lot of "should"s running the show. I *should* go to that party; I *should* make small talk. I now know Autistic people regularly use these compensatory strategies (behaviors involving forcing yourself to do unnatural things in order to appear less Autistic). One way this often shows up is by forcing yourself to socialize when you are low on social energy.

Many Autistic people have a much smaller social battery than the average person. We also may enjoy socializing less than others do. Personally, I've learned that larger gatherings, especially indoors, overwhelm my nervous system and trigger a state of freeze (low-key dissociation due to sensory overload). In such states, enjoying socializing becomes challenging, if not impossible. As part of my self-care regimen, I now prioritize social events where I can be truly present and engaged. For me, this means enjoying outdoor walks with friends, playing games with my immediate family, and connecting through email, text, and other forms that don't require a lot of people in a room together.

It also means I say no to more things, without guilt. I focus on saying yes to events that align with my social preferences. I mindfully consider my "social spoons" (in this context, spoons are energy units that represent my capacity for social interaction) and strategically invest them in meaningful interactions. You can do the same thing for your self-care plan—assess what works for you, then attend events that appeal to you and decline invitations to gatherings that create stress and discomfort.

Finally, know that it's okay to enjoy being alone—it doesn't mean anything's wrong with you if you don't need copious socializing. So go ahead and recharge that social battery and spend time doing things you enjoy! Honoring your social boundaries is essential to building healthy and fulfilling relationships.

# Manage Clashing Sensory Needs
## *Romantic Relationships*

Romantic relationships play a significant role in many of our lives, and it's essential to consider how your self-care practices can address the unique needs that arise in these relationships. Depending on your and your partner's sensory profiles, you may be working with vastly different sets of needs. For example, one partner could lean toward sensory-seeking behaviors in touch, while the other might be more sensory avoidant. Similarly, one might find comfort in sensory-seeking movements, while the other could be sensitive to sound, finding their partner's frequent movements overwhelming to their senses.

The key thing to keep in mind when sorting through sensory needs is that it's a matter of addressing clashing sensory needs, not a matter of character flaws. Without this mindset, it's easy to resort to character-based attributions, like labeling someone as "too loud" or "too sensitive." By adopting a cooperative lens, you can shift focus from assigning blame to simply recognizing the sensory dynamics involved. This shift transitions the discussion to effective problem-solving. Rather than seeing clashing sensory needs as a reflection of individual inadequacies, you can recognize it as a mutual obstacle requiring resolution.

To manage both parties' needs, consider following these steps:

1. Identify each partner's sensory needs.
2. Pinpoint high-clash areas.
3. Develop joint solutions that cater to everyone's sensory preferences.

This approach fosters a relationship that values and accommodates diverse sensory experiences and allows you to enjoy spending time with your partner. When your sensory needs are met, you'll find yourself more relaxed, grounded, and able to truly connect with your partner.

# Explore Gender and Sexuality
## *Romantic Relationships*

Autistic people tend to diverge from cis-het (cisgender-heterosexual) norms more than their allistic counterparts. For some of us, conforming to cis-het norms has been an integral aspect of our masking, making the journey to uncover our gender and sexual identities uniquely complex, especially if we discover them later in life.

Understanding your gender and sexual identities is a cornerstone for establishing meaningful and authentic romantic relationships. This exploration spans various dimensions, including gender, sexuality, relationship preferences, and engagement with kink culture.

As you unmask, consider these aspects:

- **Gender identity:** Autistic people identify as genderqueer at much higher rates than allistic people. Embracing your authentic gender identity will enrich your self-understanding and deepen your connections.

- **Sexuality:** Grasping the nuances of your sexuality and preferences will help you communicate transparently with partners. If you are queer, you may appreciate the term "neuroqueer," which refers to those of us who are neurodivergent and also queer.

- **Kink culture:** Some Autistic people find solace within kink culture. This realm offers a unique blend of playfulness and heightened sensory pleasure within the context of sexuality.

- **Polyamory versus monogamy:** Polyamory appears to be more common among Autistic people. If that resonates with you, talk with your partner early on in your relationship so that you can discuss dynamics and establish consensual agreements.

As you explore who you truly are, be gentle and patient with yourself.

# Identify Your Love Language
## *Romantic Relationships*

"Love languages" is a phrase coined by Dr. Gary Chapman in his 1992 book *The Five Love Languages: How to Express Heartfelt Commitment to Your Mate*. It describes the ways in which people prefer to give and receive love. He proposed that people have unique approaches to expressing and accepting love and suggested that when partners openly discuss these love languages, it can strengthen emotional connections and relationships.

Dr. Chapman's five love languages include:

- **Words of Affirmation:** Expressing love and appreciation through verbal compliments, praise, and encouragement.
- **Acts of Service:** Expressing love through considerate actions and kind gestures.
- **Receiving Gifts:** Feeling loved through meaningful gifts.
- **Quality Time:** Feeling loved through spending quality time and undivided attention.
- **Physical Touch:** Feeling loved through physical affection like hugs, kisses, holding hands, and other forms of touch.

As an Autistic person, however, you may find that some of these traditional love languages don't naturally align with your preferences and sensory needs. For instance, verbal Words of Affirmation can feel overwhelming for me, and I can more easily appreciate them in written form. Acts of Service might be your way of showing love, but demand avoidance or burnout can make them challenging to execute. And Receiving Gifts might be uncomfortable due to difficulty concealing emotions and the pressure to respond in an "appropriate" way to the gift giver. Quality Time can be enjoyable when balanced with alone time, and Physical Touch can be complicated depending on sensory sensitivities!

What all that boils down to is that these traditional love languages might not work for you—which is absolutely fine. You might instead possess distinct love languages that better suit your needs and journeys.

**Here are some alternative love languages to contemplate:**

- **Info swapping or info dumping:** Sharing passions and interests through passionate dialogue and engaging in shared activities or discussions related to each other's interests.

- **Parallel play:** Engaging in similar activities alongside each other without the demand for ongoing conversation.

- **Sensory comfort:** Expressing love in a sensory-friendly environment or via comfort objects.

- **Respect for boundaries:** Demonstrating love by respecting personal boundaries and sensory sensitivities.

- **Written expressions:** Writing notes to express feelings and communicate love.

- **Predictability and routine:** Demonstrating love by providing a stable and predictable environment.

Naturally, every individual is distinct. You might connect with the classic or alternative love languages, enjoy some of each, or have your own preferences altogether. What matters most is the ability to discuss how you express and experience love with your partner. Engage in open conversations so everyone is on the same page and both you and your partner can feel seen, appreciated, and happy.

# Navigate Dating Apps and Websites
## *Romantic Relationships*

Navigating dating apps has become an essential aspect of modern dating. However, it can bring about some unique challenges and anxieties for Autistic people. Questions about whether or not to disclose your autism, handling unpredictable first dates, and ensuring safety can create a whirlwind of uncertainties.

Here's a collection of tips to guide you through crafting your profile, initiating conversations, and arranging dates:

- **Consider selective self-disclosure:** If you're unsure about disclosing your autism, consider including a partial self-disclosure in your profile, such as "I am neurodivergent." This up-front approach can help you find connections with people who are accepting of your neurodivergence while also avoiding a full self-disclosure that may lead to discomfort or unnecessary pressure and discrimination.

- **Attract the right match:** The information you choose to share can shape the type of people you draw toward you. Highlight the aspects of yourself that hold the most significance and resonate with your values. Given that many Autistic people are value driven, it's likely that you'll find better compatibility with those who share your values. If you hold values that are nonnegotiable for you, consider including them on your page. For instance, you can express, "I strongly align with antiracist, queer-affirming, and anti-ableist values." This approach will ensure a more compatible connection.

- **Showcase special interests:** Many Autistic people connect deeply when discussing shared interests. Consider incorporating your interests into your profile to provide conversation starters that can foster meaningful connections with people who share your interests (bonus— this will often create an opener for more object-based conversations).

- **Minimize idealization:** Some people create idealized images of those they've connected with online. This inclination may be heightened among Autistic people, as many of us gravitate toward fantasy as a means of escape (fantasy often feels simpler than real life). Additionally, our penchant for turning a person into a special interest can lead to intense infatuation. To maintain realistic expectations, consider meeting in person relatively early on. Direct face-to-face interaction can offer a truer representation of the individual, helping you form a more accurate perception.

- **Prioritize safety:** Be vigilant about recognizing potential red flags during interactions, and have initial meetings in safe places. Autistic people can be more vulnerable to victimization because we sometimes struggle to perceive ill intentions. When engaging with someone online, prioritize safety by having initial meetings in safe places and being cautious of people offering big, exciting things, such as "fly to California and I'll make you a model!" If an interaction feels questionable, don't hesitate to ask a trusted friend for their input.

Dating can be an enjoyable and fun way to meet new people. By addressing these points, you can fully immerse yourself in the moment, allowing you to focus on the person you are meeting rather than getting caught up in the logistical aspects of the date.

# Plan a Sensory-Friendly Date
## *Romantic Relationships*

You want dating to be fun and relaxing. But as an Autistic person, you also need to recognize the intricate connection between your sensory and social systems. Sensory overload can trigger stress responses in your nervous system, leading to either hyperarousal or hypoarousal states. In both cases, your social system goes offline, and with it, your ability to engage meaningfully with a partner. You might feel distant and detached, while your date might feel as if they aren't truly connecting with you.

For this reason, it is critical to consider the sensory environment of your first date, especially because first dates can be anxiety inducing to begin with!

Here are some ideas for sensory-friendly dates:

- **Nature outings:** If the weather permits, exploring a natural setting through an activity like hiking, kayaking, biking along a scenic route, birdwatching in a local park, or stargazing on a clear night can provide a unique opportunity for connection. Nature's calming effect can significantly regulate sensory experiences for many Autistic people, making it an ideal backdrop for meaningful interactions.

- **Intimate cafés and restaurants:** Opt for quiet and dimly lit cafés and restaurants. These settings create a cozy ambience that minimizes sensory overload and fosters comfortable conversation.

- **Stress-free walks:** Going for a walk can be an excellent choice. Walking offers built-in sensory regulation as it provides a rhythmic movement, which can be soothing. Additionally, walking naturally reduces the pressure of sustained eye contact, a common sensory demand.

- **Creative workshops or classes:** Consider engaging in a creative activity together—such as a painting class, pottery workshop, or cooking class—which provides a built-in form of parallel play. These environments invite opportunities for interaction while keeping the focus on the activity, which can ease social stress.

- **Outdoor picnics:** A picnic in a calm outdoor location can be a great alternative to a busy restaurant. You have control over the sensory environment, allowing for a more relaxed and sensory-friendly atmosphere.

- **Botanical gardens or arboretums:** Exploring the vibrant colors, textures, and scents of a botanical garden or arboretum can be a grounding but sensory-rich and relaxing experience. These environments offer serene backdrops for conversation and connection while being "event" related, reducing some of the social pressures.

Brainstorming and suggesting date locations that work for you is a proactive way to create an environment that fosters genuine connection and meaningful engagement. That way, you can focus on determining if this person is a good match for you.

# Find Sensory Accommodations for Sexual Intimacy

*Romantic Relationships*

Sex is a highly sensory experience, creating unique challenges for many Autistic people. From demands for eye contact to bodily contact and the array of sensory experiences in between, navigating these aspects can be daunting.

In the same way that you accommodate your sensory needs in other areas of your life, it is just as important to consider ways of accommodating your sensory needs when it comes to your intimate life. This not only enhances your comfort and pleasure but also strengthens your connection with your partner.

However, addressing these considerations with partners can often stir feelings of insecurity and anxiety, leading to hesitance in initiating these conversations or avoiding them altogether. Nevertheless, an important part of your social self-care is communicating these needs to your partner. After all, each partner's comfort is essential for an enjoyable and meaningful sexual experience. While it might seem awkward to bring up, addressing these matters is the best option for the long-term strength of your relationship.

Here are a few accommodations to consider:

- **Touch:** Autistic people often have strong preferences around touch (firm versus soft). Communicating touch preferences can help your partner provide enjoyable touch within your comfort zone.

- **Clothing:** During a workshop exploring the intersection of kink culture and autism, a participant mused about whether garments linked to kink culture might serve as a "second skin," adding tactile protection during intimacy. If that resonates with you, consider whether certain garments could help make your experience better.

- **Body boundaries:** Establishing body boundaries is crucial for your sense of physical and emotional safety. Defining these boundaries, whether it's the amount of physical contact or specific areas to avoid, supports a respectful and pleasurable experience for both partners.

- **Eye contact:** Openly discussing the desired or undesired levels of eye contact during moments of intimacy can help reduce discomfort and allow both partners to feel at ease. For a playful approach, consider experimenting with blindfolds if this is within your comfort zone.

- **Lighting:** Lighting plays a significant role in sensory experiences. Opting for no lighting or dimmed lighting can greatly reduce your overall sensory load, providing more bandwidth for other sensory experiences.

- **Music:** While adding music may be too overstimulating for some, for others, a stim song may serve as a grounding function and provide a supportive addition.

These accommodations don't need to be static—you can use trial and error to see what works best and make changes as needed. This collaborative journey toward mutual pleasure and understanding can bring you even closer to your partner.

# Build Emotional Intimacy
## Romantic Relationships

Navigating the path to emotional intimacy can pose some unique challenges for Autistic people, especially if you also have alexithymia (refer to Grasp Difficult Emotions in Chapter 3). Cross-neurotype relationships can make the situation even more complex.

**Here are key considerations for nurturing deeper emotional connections with your partner:**

- **Identify what types of connections you value most:** Emotional connection varies widely, especially across different neurotypes. For instance, my intellectual connection with someone often feels like a profound emotional bond. However, I've noticed this experience is less common among allistic people, who tend to differentiate intellectual and emotional connections. Many allistic people tend to prefer using emotionally rich and socially based language to build emotional connections. Initiating a dialogue with your partner about which types of conversations make you both feel emotionally connected is a crucial starting point.

- **Explore different communication mediums:** If verbally articulating intense emotions proves challenging, explore alternative ways to share your inner world. Composing letters, expressing yourself through art, or sharing meaningful songs can serve as an alternative channel for conveying your feelings. Moreover, this approach can act as an "emotional prompt" that encourages your partner to ask questions so you can further explore your inner world together.

- **Do activities together:** Engaging in activities that hold emotional significance for both partners generates shared moments of emotional closeness.

- **Know your limit:** It's essentially impossible to be emotionally connected when you're flooded, which is a state of emotional overload where it becomes challenging to think or communicate clearly. And Autistic people become flooded more easily! Recognizing your threshold and temporarily stepping away from the conversation until you're ready to reengage is crucial for maintaining healthy interactions.

- **Adapt "active listening":** It is well-known that active listening is very important in relationships—paying close attention to what someone says and being able to reflect it back to them empowers us to grasp differing viewpoints and validate emotions. Nevertheless, practicing active listening can sometimes overwhelm the Autistic system, ironically diminishing the effectiveness of this very practice. If sustained eye contact proves taxing, consider shifting conversations to a walking setting, making active listening more manageable. Alternatively, you may find that your active listening flourishes during parallel tactile activities like baking or shared doodling.

- **Reflect and communicate:** Dedicate consistent time for open conversation. Engaging in discussions about the evolution of emotional needs and changing preferences as your relationship advances can deepen your connection. Consider incorporating questions encouraging self-reflection, such as "What is one new thing I learned about myself in our interactions this week?" and "What is a small change we can make to enhance our connection?" This practice can establish a structured space for open dialogue, creating an expected ritual and routine.

By recognizing the distinct strengths and challenges in neurodiverse partnerships, you lay the foundation for cultivating emotional intimacy. You can achieve emotional closeness by being open with your partner about your emotional landscape.

# Resolve Conflict in Relationships
## Romantic Relationships

Navigating conflict in relationships is complex, especially in neurodiverse partnerships (in this context, neurodiverse means two different neurotypes are involved). Adding to this, conflicts can easily overwhelm Autistic people due to our heightened sensory and nervous systems, resulting in conflict avoidance.

Here are key points to consider when addressing conflict:

Communication Basics

- **Consider neurodiversity:** Varying communication styles can lead to misunderstandings. Approach conflict with an openness to comprehend and learn from each other's perspectives.

- **Practice clear and direct communication:** Express your viewpoint and feelings clearly, and also actively listen to your partner's perspective. Allow both parties uninterrupted time to voice concerns. If your partner communicates indirectly, support their growth in direct communication with patience as they refine this skill.

- **Use an open-dialogue format:** Foster an environment where both partners feel secure sharing thoughts and emotions. Keep in mind that Autistic people often face challenges in tone modulation and recognition. If your partner perceives your tone as harsh, consider this feedback. Likewise, your partner should recognize tone modulation difficulties as a part of your Autistic experience.

## Navigating Sensory and Emotional Overload

- **Manage your nervous system:** Renowned couples therapist Dr. John Gottman employed a unique strategy involving partners wearing heartbeat-monitoring devices (like smartwatches). If one partner's heartbeat surpassed a specific threshold, the conversation halted. Dr. Gottman knew that effective communication wanes beyond a certain stress level. This example is valuable because it provides couples with a tangible reminder to stop when things get heated! Additionally, it's crucial to be aware of "faux regulation," which your partner might not recognize as stress. Faux regulation occurs when you seem calm but are actually in a state of stress—such as the freeze-fawn mode (see Understand Your Body's Responses to Stress in Chapter 2).

- **Take time-outs:** Understand when sensory or emotional overload is at play. Agree on signals for time-outs if either of you is feeling overwhelmed.

- **Account for sensory considerations:** Factor in sensory sensitivities. Choose a comfortable, quiet space to discuss conflicts, minimizing sensory triggers.

## Collaborative Problem-Solving

- **Define the issue:** Clearly state the problem to prevent confusion (note that in cross-neurotype conflicts, differing definitions of the issue can be common, making clarity crucial as a starting point!).

- **Brainstorm solutions:** Generate ideas together, prioritizing compromises that honor both parties' needs.

- **Implement agreements:** Act on jointly agreed-upon solutions, periodically evaluating their effectiveness and doing regular check-ins.

Disagreements aren't fun—but they are unavoidable. Honoring your neurodiversity and being intentional in your communication can deepen mutual understanding and help you navigate conflicts more constructively.

# Embrace an Aromantic
# or Asexual Identity
## Romantic Relationships

There is an outdated stereotype that Autistic people can't be sexual or romantic. And while this stereotype comes from antiquated and ableist thinking about autism, it is also important to acknowledge that many of us do identify as asexual and/or aromantic (sometimes referred to as ace/aro or the ace/aro spectrum).

The ace/aro spectrum encompasses a broad array of orientations, spanning from asexuality (lack of sexual attraction) to aromanticism (lack of romantic feelings) to demisexuality (partial or conditional sexual attraction based on intense emotional connection). It's important to know that many people who identify as asexual or aromantic still seek profound connections. For example, they might be drawn to enduring platonic partnerships.

Embarking on a journey of self-discovery while embracing your ace/aro identity can be an empowering process, particularly if your Autistic mask once projected a sexualized version of yourself. For some, sensory sensitivities can complicate physical relationships, and you might be in the process of determining what is sensory aversion and what might be an ace/aro identity. If you've just learned about your autism, you might want to take that opportunity to dissect your identity, differentiate sensory needs from your genuine self, and unravel the influences of your mask on your sexual history and inclinations.

Traditional cultural and societal narratives often disregard ace/aro identities, which can feel isolating. Remember that forging meaningful connections is a unique path without one single right way. Prioritize self-care by not judging yourself based on societal expectations but instead embracing and loving yourself for who you are.

# CHAPTER SIX

• • •

# Professional Self-Care

Integrating your Autistic identity and professional life is a powerful way to reduce the energy you expend on masking and mitigate overexertion. For many of us, the cycle of working, collapsing, and repeating is all too familiar.

Unfortunately, Autistic people face disproportionately high rates of unemployment and underemployment, a trend that resonates with the challenges many of us experience in navigating work environments. From our distinct cognitive processing styles to sensory sensitivities, numerous factors can make workplace dynamics difficult to navigate. In some cases, a lack of confidence may lead us to settle for roles beneath our potential, while others grapple with impostor syndrome, perfectionism, and the desire to please, often leading to burnout and crash cycles! For all these reasons, it's crucial to focus some of your self-care efforts on your professional world.

Interestingly, many late-in-life-identified Autistic people reconsider their career paths in the wake of this revelation. As we begin to construct lives that work for us, I've noticed that many of us shift toward careers that align with our interests and support our sensory well-being.

In this chapter, you'll find activities divided into a few key categories: navigating the workplace, creating an optimal work environment, and finding executive functioning support. You'll learn strategies for crafting a work environment tailored to your strengths and preferences. Topics include navigating self-disclosure in professional settings, advocating for accommodations, managing sensory sensitivities, and capitalizing on Autistic strengths. Your skills, ideas, and work ethic make you an important asset to your workplace—the entries in this chapter will make sure your workplace is a beneficial part of your life as well.

# Selectively Share Your
# Autistic Identity with Colleagues
## *Workplace Tips*

A common cause of stress is whether to reveal your Autistic identity within a professional environment.

When contemplating self-disclosure in the workplace, here are some considerations:

- Clarify your motives: Reflect on why you'd share your autism with others. Is it to establish authentic connections with colleagues? Do you want people to understand your actions better? Are you seeking accommodations? Understanding the motivations behind self-disclosure and your hoped-for outcome can help guide your decision.

- Determine who needs to know: While you might inform human resources about your diagnosis, not everyone at work needs this info. Certain managers may need to know in order to implement accommodations you qualify for; however, getting accommodations doesn't automatically grant your entire workplace access to your diagnosis (this information is typically protected, depending on your workplace protocols). To know who has access, inquire with human resources during the accommodations process.

- Identify how much you need to share: Carefully evaluate which alterations in your environment could improve your quality of life (such as wearing a hat to mitigate lighting, relocating to minimize exposure to strong scents, or requesting softer lighting), and subsequently, consider the level of self-disclosure necessary to effectively convey these needs. You're not obligated to divulge everything (for insights into partial versus full self-disclosure, see Decide Whether to Tell People You Are Autistic in Chapter 5).

- **Assess the risks:** There are inherent risks regardless of your choice. If you choose not to disclose, coworkers might speculate about your behavior without proper context, leading to potentially misconstrued narratives. Conversely, if you do decide to disclose, people might interpret your actions through the lens of autism stereotypes, and this could include doubting your capability for certain tasks. For instance, in my field, the misconception that Autistic people can't be good therapists still persists! Therefore, a therapist in training may opt to carefully weigh the potential consequences of sharing this information with a supervisor. There is no risk-free path, so it is wise to weigh the risks thoughtfully.

Your decision to self-disclose professionally is personal and context dependent. Your professional goals are an important part of your life, so consider what choices will make your workdays less stressful, more in line with your values, and ultimately more fulfilling.

# Navigate Context Shifting in the Workplace
## Workplace Tips

In the ever-evolving world of workplaces, grappling with neurotypical culture's intricacies can trigger anxiety. Context shifting in the workplace is often demanding and can involve the art of smoothly transitioning across a wide range of tasks, communication styles, and expectations. Plus, you're also navigating social interactions along with juggling professional duties.

Allistic people possess an innate ability to absorb context cues subcortically—meaning their brains intuitively pick up these subtle differences, which allows them to effortlessly grasp context signals. On the other hand, Autistic people are more context independent, embodying authenticity across situations and contexts. We don't inherently absorb context cues as seamlessly as our allistic peers do. Instead, we need to mobilize our prefrontal cortexes to analyze situations.

For example, say there's a team meeting where everyone appears engaged, but there's an unspoken tension in the room. Autistic people might not immediately grasp this undercurrent because it's not explicitly communicated. Instead, we might need to consciously analyze the situation, observing body language, tone, and other context cues to decipher the dynamics. This process demands significant mental effort and can be mentally draining.

This can make it tricky to navigate traditional workplaces. Regrettably, our difficulty with automatically picking up subtle context cues related to authority, hierarchy, and professionalism can lead to misinterpretation. In certain cases, this misinterpretation can even result in premature job terminations and erroneous blame for unprofessional conduct.

If you find yourself in the throes of context shifting in your workplace, here are some tips:

- **Ask for explicit guidance:** Seek direct guidance on workplace norms and rules, particularly in scenarios where the context shifts. If, for instance, colleagues frequently dine together or there are workplace holiday events, inquire about the explicit rules that underlie these shifts.

- **Observe and learn:** I honed my context-cue skills by becoming a mini social scientist during childhood. Likewise, if you become an amateur social scientist in the workplace, you might find yourself better able to decode the context norms. Study your colleagues' communication patterns, body language, and strategies. If you're comfortable, discuss subtle shifts you've noticed with someone you trust. Observing neurotypicals within their natural habitat is a great way to learn about their intricacies.

- **Seek support:** Don't hesitate to seek guidance from mentors, peers, or supervisors. Consider requesting a mentor, especially if you're openly Autistic at work, who can be your go-to person for Autistic-allistic queries. Collaborating with an allistic person to help you decode the subtleties can take some of the guesswork out of it!

Remember, context shifting is exhausting work, and context decoding often involves an element of masking, which negatively impacts mental health and energy levels for Autistic people. Perhaps the best way to address this is to choose a field that is more Autistic friendly. Fields like tech, STEM fields, medicine, and academia are often more innately Autistic friendly. Additionally, many Autistic people find relief when they're able to work remotely. If your workplace isn't currently Autistic friendly, however, try the tips in this entry and be sure to take care of your body and mind as you do.

# Document Everything
## *Workplace Tips*

Autistic people's direct communication style and optimism can make us more susceptible to exploitation within certain systems or situations. Navigating these dynamics demands a proactive approach, and consistent documentation can help you assert your stance during conflicts and provide a record that creates some safeguard from unjust blame.

Your documentation does not need to be intricate. A basic word processing document, notes app, or email program can serve as an effective tool. Describe conversations as accurately as your memory allows.

Here are some documenting tips for keeping track of situations and events so you're prepared:

- Capture conversations and agreements as factual reference points.
- Note pivotal points, decisions, and agreements.
- Provide chronological context with date, time, and location.
- Capture the essence of what was said in concise summaries.
- Preserve relevant email trails. In addition, consider sending follow-up emails summarizing key points of conversation to be sure everyone's on the same page.

Documenting empowers you, shaping your narrative and strengthening your stance, especially should you ever need to CYA (cover your ass). Plus, it can build self-confidence and conviction in the workplace and help you feel more in control.

# Ditch Perfectionism
## *Workplace Tips*

Autistic people often possess intensely focused minds. While this can manifest as brilliance in areas of passion, it also presents challenges. For instance, minor design details can pull us into hyperfixation mode. This heightened focus and these high standards can also drive us to perfectionism, causing distress, fatigue, and overworking.

Here are practices you can employ to liberate yourself from the grip of perfectionism:

- **Embrace the practice of "good enough" work:** This will be a gradual process that you should try a little at a time. Try to purposefully submit work that meets your "good enough" standard (not your "perfect" standard), gradually desensitizing yourself to the distress and stress that may accompany it. With each iteration, the "good enough" work becomes more manageable. Consider it a process of strengthening your resilience muscle against the pressure of delivering flawless outcomes.

- **Embrace feedback:** Ask your boss which details genuinely contribute to the bigger picture. Given our tendency to delve into specifics, an external perspective can help you gauge where you should focus your time and energy.

- **Master mindfulness:** Cultivate mindfulness to stay rooted in the present moment. When your mind conjures perfectionistic scripts, practice identifying and naming them. This simple act can help diminish the mental clutter that fuels perfectionist tendencies.

By aiming to let go of perfectionism, you can forge a more balanced, sustainable work journey while leveraging your inherent strengths. This plan will help you reduce stress and make your job more enjoyable.

# Ask for Examples
## *Workplace Tips*

In college and graduate school, one of the first things I'd do when assigned a new project was google for examples. I always really appreciated when professors provided examples from previous years. Here's the thing: I often didn't know where to start without visual context for what was being asked of me! Having examples can be immensely helpful for Autistic people, and this tip is especially valuable in the workplace.

Here are some of the ways an example can help support you:

- It clarifies the instructions: Allistic people often provide vague directions. Having an example can help clarify what is being asked.

- It provides visual context: Autistic people often thrive on visual learning; information presented in a visual context carries more meaning and understanding. Plus, visual examples provide an anchor for your comprehension. They offer a concrete representation of what's expected, making it easier to process, absorb, and execute tasks accurately.

- It helps with sequencing: Sequencing the steps to get from one point to another can be difficult for Autistic people. Seeing an example can help us to sequence the actions needed to complete the task.

- It can save hours of potential frustration, sweat, and anxiety: A visual model significantly reduces the need for trial and error and wasted effort.

- It enhances productivity: By seeking examples, you're not just accommodating your learning style—you're building a bridge between your understanding and the task at hand. This bridge minimizes the potential for errors and ensures that your contributions align with the expectations.

Advocating for yourself and asking for examples clearly has lots of benefits, both for you and your employer.

**Here are some things to keep in mind when asking for examples:**

- Connect your request to an underlying need. Express your preference for visual learning and your interest in examples.

- If you're tasked with a specific project, inquire if there's a template available or a previous similar example. Templates often provide structured frameworks, while previous examples offer practical guides.

- When requesting examples, be specific about the type of guidance you're seeking. For example, ask for last year's document, a step-by-step illustration, or a reference of similar work.

By requesting examples, you're not only advocating for yourself but also contributing to a more inclusive work environment for all employees. This proactive approach cultivates inclusivity because it promotes a culture of collaboration and support. Your pursuit of visual clarity might even inspire others to adopt similar practices, creating a workplace where diverse learning styles are embraced!

# Succeed at Job Interviewing
## *Workplace Tips*

For many Autistic people, job interviews don't exactly showcase our full potential! The conventional interview setting can induce anxiety as it frequently depends on spontaneity and rapid processing. We often thrive as deep processors, benefitting from ample time to formulate thoughtful responses. The interview landscape, often devoid of contextual familiarity and spontaneity, can be disorienting.

Here are some tips that can help make the process less stressful and better allow you to showcase your skills:

- **Practice:** Repeated practice is your ally. Search online for commonly asked interview questions and rehearse your responses. If you are primed for some of the questions ahead of time, you can prepare your answers and respond more confidently.

- **Craft compelling stories:** Compile an arsenal of stories or examples that reflect your problem-solving skills, creativity, and/or determination. It's likely easier to think of these ahead of time than on the spot, and they can become responses to many types of questions.

- **Use strategic pauses:** If rapid-fire responses aren't in your comfort zone, develop a few strategic statements, such as "That's an insightful question; let me gather my thoughts for a moment." This tactical pause gives your mind a moment to process and structure a response.

- **Get contextual clarity:** Having context about the company can help you anchor yourself in the interview. Research the company, its values, and its mission ahead of time. This background knowledge can help you build a conceptual map for the company, resulting in you feeling more grounded.

- **Try mirror and mock interviews:** Practice in front of a mirror or involve a trusted friend for mock interviews. Insights from a friend can illuminate unnoticed elements—spanning body language to tone—aiding you in refining your interview demeanor. Another valuable technique is recording yourself with a voice memo and reviewing it. This tactic has proven effective for me in refining my tone and speech pace and reinforcing word memory.

- **Consider your posture:** Posture, an essential element of nonverbal communication, can often lead to misunderstandings and misjudgments for Autistic people. Many of us unintentionally display a flat affect that might be misconstrued as disinterest. Ask a trusted friend or mentor to help you find a posture that's physically comfortable yet signals openness.

- **Find accommodations for eye contact:** Eye contact can be particularly tricky, as many interviewers expect it. You can experiment with eye contact techniques, like focusing between the interviewer's eyes, subtly conveying engagement while reducing discomfort.

Interviews often trigger anxiety, and they also compel you to grapple with the dilemma of masking versus unmasking. Your approach will hinge on your personal choice and circumstances.

Regardless, practice and preparation enable you to find a balanced approach of embracing your genuine identity while feeling at ease during interviews, allowing your authentic self to shine through.

# Compare Bottom-Up Thinking versus Top-Down Thinking
## Workplace Tips

Part of what it means to be neurodivergent is that the way we process information diverges from that of neurotypical brains. In the context of the workplace, it can be helpful to understand these different cognitive patterns. Recognizing your unique processing style and how it diverges from the allistic norm can maximize your comfort and productivity in the workplace.

Among the diverse modes of processing, one that distinctly characterizes Autistic brains is bottom-up processing. Bottom-up processing involves an immersive and methodical journey through the nuances of information. Unlike top-down processing, which weaves a few pivotal pieces of data into a coherent whole, bottom-up processing delves into the minute details, meticulously piecing them together to construct a comprehensive understanding. This approach enables Autistic people to forge intricate connections and associations between various elements, cultivating a deep understanding of complex systems.

However, this detailed-oriented approach is a double-edged sword. While it facilitates deep comprehension, it demands substantial cognitive resources. The misnomer of "slow processing" often misrepresents the reality—Autistic people are actually deep processors. This depth necessitates more time, making our initial onboarding into new concepts or systems slower. This initial investment, however, is well worth it and serves us and our workplaces well. Once we immerse ourselves in the intricacies of a subject, our understanding is not only profound but also multifaceted and robust.

In navigating your strengths and challenges in the workplace, the bottom-up cognitive approach presents both advantages and hurdles. Its meticulous nature can be mentally taxing, potentially leading to exhaustion. However, this bottom-up processing style also empowers you to offer thorough and intricate solutions to complex problems.

Acknowledging and embracing this cognitive style can help you lean into your strengths while also encouraging you to be compassionate with yourself when your processing pace differs from those around you. Your eventual mastery will help you build confidence, ultimately enriching the overall landscape of the workplace.

Across your workplace, you might see both bottom-up and top-down thinking. This diversity fosters a dynamic and creative workforce, ultimately enhancing the overall quality of your workplace experience. Taking care of yourself by acknowledging your cognitive style and celebrating its contributions is a crucial aspect of your professional well-being.

# Find a Mentor to Show You the Ropes
## *Workplace Tips*

During my training to become a psychologist, each year I switched between new work environments, such as hospital clinics and college universities. This shift brought both the stress of adapting to new systems and rules and the challenge of fitting into subtle cultural norms.

In these fresh work settings, I grappled with numerous questions, feeling embarrassed about seeking help. It was difficult to find a balance between not wanting to burden specific individuals and obtaining assistance from those I felt at ease with! This struggle could have been ameliorated with a mentor's support, because that person could have helped guide me through the complexities of new systems.

Entering a new workplace involves more than filling out forms and setting up your computer—the underlying work culture, often overlaid with unspoken rules and practices, is equally significant. Decoding this hidden layer, typically learned implicitly through observation and interactions, can be particularly demanding for Autistic people and can cause frustration and confusion. One way to alleviate this stress is to find a mentor, someone who can illuminate these unwritten codes and provide insights into the implicit aspects of work culture.

Mentors can be formally assigned by your workplace or found informally through individuals you naturally connect with. If you are openly Autistic in the workplace, consider requesting a formal mentor as part of your accommodation requests. If not, consider asking someone you connect with to be your informal mentor as you learn the ropes.

Mentorship has the potential to enhance not only your understanding of work culture but also your personal and professional growth. Plus, this mentor can lower stress levels, help you believe in yourself, and allow you to thrive in your workplace.

# Manage Overstimulation at Work
## *Optimal Work Environments*

The workplace can be a breeding ground for overstimulation. When you're overstimulated, you're not going to be able to focus or work effectively. Managing your sensory environment becomes critical to cultivating a workplace in which you can thrive. I often call the perfect stimulus range the "Goldilocks zone," where I'm not understimulated or overstimulated. If you're an AuDHDer (Autistic ADHDer) like me, you'll understand this challenge! Discovering your Goldilocks zone is key for unlocking focus.

Here are some tailored strategies to consider:

- **Find a quiet retreat:** Request access to a dedicated quiet space. This can help counteract the overwhelming sensory input of a busy office.

- **Consider listening to music:** My favorite is having a repeat stim song playing in one earbud. This can create a sensory buffer without compromising awareness of the surroundings.

- **Schedule breaks:** Take short breaks to step away and recalibrate when sensory input overwhelms you.

- **Adjust your environment:** Modify lighting, seating, or desk arrangement to minimize sensory triggers.

- **Assemble a sensory tool kit:** Curate a sensory tool kit with items that soothe and regulate your sensory system, such as fidget toys, a weighted lap pad, or noise-canceling headphones.

By making these adjustments, you can cultivate a work environment that better aligns with your sensory needs. Plus, most of them are at low or no cost for your employer, making this a win-win situation. You'll find yourself calmer, more focused, and happier as you work.

# Find Accommodations That Work
## *Optimal Work Environments*

Accommodations might sound complex, but they can be surprisingly simple. For instance, I wear a beanie daily. While it might not look conventionally professional, the firm pressure provides sensory comfort and helps me regulate my body with more ease. Others may benefit from brimmed hats that block overhead light glare. Accommodations can also be more formal requests that go through human resources.

You may have legal rights to accommodations depending on your location and diagnosis status. In the United States, autism is protected under the Americans with Disabilities Act, ensuring reasonable accommodations.

Here are some accommodation ideas to consider:

- Sensory breaks
- Dedicated, focused work time
- Flexible work schedules for remote work
- Clear, direct, written feedback
- Noise-reducing workspace
- Ability to use noise-canceling headphones
- Adjustable lighting
- Use of fidget tools
- Reduced open-plan office exposure
- Access to a quiet zone
- Regular check-ins with a designated support person
- Flexible communication accommodating various preferences
- Advanced warning of schedule changes
- Providing a consistent routine and clear expectations

To discover accommodations and learn more, visit the Job Accommodation Network (JAN). They provide comprehensive workplace information and a searchable accommodation database. Accommodations like these can foster productivity, focus, creativity, and a sense of security at work.

# Reduce Task Switching
## *Optimal Work Environments*

"Task switching" refers to the act of stopping one task, saving its progress, and starting another, and it has a profound impact on your productivity and energy reserves. For example, if you're working on a report and then switch to answering emails or engaging in small talk with a colleague, that's a task switch.

Although the switch might be brief—perhaps taking a mere five minutes to respond to an incoming message—the aftermath of returning to the writing flow and mentally shifting back into the context of your project consumes precious time. Studies have shown that each task switch can cost you several minutes of focus!

For Autistic people, task switching is even more challenging compared to those with neurotypical brains (this is related to hyper- and hypoconnectivity in our brains). Our distinct cognitive processing makes transitioning between tasks more demanding.

Consider these strategies to mitigate task switching and ease the task-switching time drain:

- **Group similar tasks together:** Concentrating on related tasks in one session minimizes the need for frequent context shifts.

- **Manage your notifications:** Disable notifications during focused work periods. Uninterrupted concentration allows for deeper engagement without succumbing to constant task switching.

- **Request formal accommodations:** Consider requesting formal accommodations that can provide protected time, shielding you from distractions and task-switching pressures.

Minimizing task switching throughout your day enables you to immerse yourself in the deep, restorative, and creatively fulfilling work. Creating this space for focused work can lead to a more enjoyable and satisfying workday.

# Set SMART Goals
## Executive Functioning

Autistic brains tend to struggle to transition from one activity to another or to start new tasks (commonly referred to as task initiation). One factor that can hinder task initiation is related to executive functioning issues.

One effective strategy to overcome this hurdle is to break tasks down into their smallest components. For instance, when I struggled to begin working on writing this book, the smallest step was simply grabbing my computer and opening the document I wrote this book in. When I can get myself to do the first step, I can typically enter a flow state and start writing. The hardest part is starting!

The concept of SMART goals provides a structured approach for breaking tasks down into smaller elements. The SMART approach—creating goals that are specific, measurable, achievable, relevant, and time-bound—acts as a framework for effective goal setting that can be applied to both your personal and professional lives. This method is particularly useful when tackling large workplace goals that are initially broad or long-term.

- Specific: Clearly define your desired outcome by being precise and detailed, avoiding vague intentions like "be better at my job" or "get healthier." Instead, pinpoint exactly what you want, like "learn how to use a new software."

- Measurable: Make your goal measurable with specific criteria, attaching numbers or metrics. This adds tangibility—like aiming to complete three online courses or send out ten job applications.

- Achievable: Set realistic and attainable goals considering your capabilities, available resources, and potential challenges. While it's important to challenge yourself, you want the goals to be within reach and aligned with your abilities and circumstances. This approach is more empowering and increases your chances of sticking with the goals.

- **Relevant:** Align your goals with your values, aspirations, and long-term plans. If your overarching goal is to get a job, then a relevant SMART goal might be to send out five job applications.

- **Time-bound:** Establish deadlines or target dates for achieving your goals. This creates a sense of urgency, keeps you focused, and promotes accountability. Setting a time frame, such as completing five job applications in a week, provides structure that helps keep you on track.

SMART goals provide a practical way to tackle extensive projects by creating a clear road map. Keep your goals under regular review, making tweaks as needed and celebrating progress along the way. Dividing larger objectives into smaller, doable tasks keeps you motivated while supporting steady progress. Achieving these smaller benchmarks can build confidence, relieve stress, and motivate you to create new goals as well.

# Create Hyperfocus Bumper Rails
## Executive Functioning

When it comes to productivity, hyperfocus can be a double-edged sword. On one hand, it can propel you into a state of flow, where your brain operates at peak performance, fostering enhanced focus, creativity, and deep engagement. This flow state can significantly boost your cognitive abilities, increase calming brain waves, and enhance your overall well-being.

However, hyperfocus also presents its own set of challenges. While in its grasp, it can monopolize your attention and time, potentially disrupting your sleep, derailing your ability to prioritize important tasks, and creating imbalances in your work-life harmony. For instance, in my life it can lead to moments where I unintentionally neglect family and personal life, disrupt my sleep patterns, and disregard the maintenance and mundane aspects of my work! Over time, these consequences can manifest as burnout, strained relationships, sleep disturbances, and work difficulties.

Navigating hyperfocus involves finding a balance and taking control of your focus. Think of it like setting gentle rail guards to keep your hyperfocus on the right track while maintaining a healthy work-life equilibrium. This way, you can harness the benefits of deep, passionate engagement without letting it overshadow other crucial aspects of your life or work.

- **Create an exit strategy:** Set an exit plan if you anticipate engaging in an activity that triggers hyperfocus. This may include using alarms, involving another person, or intentionally scheduling a hyperfocused activity at a specific time of day.

- **Schedule hyperfocus blocks:** If you know you are someone who can work well with hyperfocus, try and protect time blocks in your work schedule for this. For example, I rarely schedule meetings on Wednesday and "gift" myself with one hyperfocus day a week. For other people, it may look like scheduling one three-hour block a day of uninterrupted work time.

- **Use reminders and timers:** Employ alarms or timers to stay mindful of the time and transition away from hyperfocus projects when necessary. Set reminders to take breaks, engage in other activities, and attend to essential tasks.

- **Engage in mindful moments:** Shifting your focus away can be challenging. If you struggle with shifting your attention when timers go off, utilize the timer slightly differently—use it as a prompt for a mindful moment. When the timer alerts you, take a brief pause and ask yourself, "Is this what I want to be doing right now?" The goal is to increase your agency and intentional decision-making. This practice cultivates awareness and creates space for intentional transitions, allowing you greater control over your choices.

Managing hyperfocus is about finding a healthy balance that allows you to enjoy your interests while attending to other important aspects of your life. By incorporating strategies and mindful practices, you can navigate hyperfocus in a way that supports balance and harmony.

# Overcome Autistic Inertia
## *Executive Functioning*

Inertia, a concept that states objects in motion tend to stay in motion while objects at rest tend to stay at rest, has been cleverly adapted to describe the challenges Autistic people face in stopping or starting tasks. This stop-and-go struggle is often referred to as "Autistic inertia."

When we're struggling to start new tasks, it can feel like there's a wave of resistance to getting started or shifting focus. However, some strategies can help you overcome Autistic inertia.

- **Break tasks into smaller steps:** Divvying a large project into manageable chunks can make it less overwhelming and easier to approach.

- **Utilize external cues:** Visual cues or alarms can prompt you to initiate or transition between tasks. These cues provide structure and direct your attention, for example, signaling the start of an activity.

- **Incorporate preferred activities and special interests:** By infusing elements of enjoyment and passion, you can tap into intrinsic motivation, making it easier to overcome inertia and engage in the task at hand. For instance, if you're passionate about presenting data in highly visual and accessible ways, you might infuse your reports with engaging visualizations and explore complex datasets.

- **Try the five-minute rule:** Set a five-minute timer and commit to working on the task for five minutes (permitting yourself to stop when the timer goes off). The key is to overcome the initial resistance by committing to five minutes, and often you find that once you start, it becomes easier to continue.

By learning to harness your natural inertia and align yourself with the current rather than fighting against it, you can unlock your creative potential and dive into deep processing. This approach leads to a more enriching and expansive work experience.

# Index

## A

Ableism, 54, 78, 94–95, 156, 166
Acceptance, 21, 78–81, 90–93, 106–7, 115, 139–43, 154–57
Acceptance and commitment therapy (ACT), 106, 124
ADHD, 9, 61, 104, 106, 126, 181
Affect labeling, 80–81
Aggression, 66–67
Alexithymia, 66–67, 74–75, 80–81, 162–63
Alone time, 112, 151, 154
Anxiety, 15–21, 29–52, 54–62, 80–92, 104–29, 138–60, 170–77
Apology reflex, 70, 95
Applied behavior analysis (ABA), 109
Art, 91–93, 139, 161–62
"Artificial skin," 68–69
Asexual/aromantic spectrum, 166
Authenticity, 22, 63, 66, 101, 115, 131–53, 168–77
Autism spectrum disorder (ASD), 109
Autistic culture, 93, 108, 136, 138–39
Autistic identity, 9–13, 92–103, 106–15, 131, 142–44, 153, 166–69
Autistic mindset, 92–94, 102–3, 108–9, 112–17, 148–52
Avoidance, 81–83, 89–91, 154, 156, 160–61, 164–65
Avoidant/Restrictive Food Intake Disorder (ARFID), 50

## B

Balance, 15–19, 24–33, 71–78, 88–91, 116–29, 154–55, 180–87
Biases, 76, 118, 122–23

BIPOC people, 13, 62, 111, 147
Body awareness, 16–18, 23, 30–33, 38, 44–49, 80
Body care, 23, 44–52. See also Self-care
Body scan, 16, 48–49, 80
Body signals, 14–20, 45, 48–49, 56–57, 80
Boundaries, 13, 19, 27, 51–57, 62–71, 144–45, 151, 155, 161
Brain dumps, 60–61, 72
Breathwork, 27, 30–37, 85, 125
Brook, Dr. Amara, 146
Burnout, 9–13, 53–61, 96–97, 114, 154, 167, 186
Busy minds, 38, 40–41

## C

Challenges, handling, 12–15, 20–22, 24–52, 54–91, 93–129, 131–66, 168–88
Chapman, Dr. Gary, 154
Checklists, using, 18, 45, 60–61
Childhood experiences, 112, 140, 171
Cognitive behavioral therapy (CBT), 106, 120
Cognitive distortions, 88, 122–25
Cognitive shuffling, 40–41
Communication, 8–22, 24–52, 54–91, 93–129, 131–65, 168–88
Confirmation bias, 76, 118
Conflict, handling, 148, 164–65
Connections, making, 8–9, 22, 102–3, 130–43, 151–69
Context shifting, 147, 170–71, 183
Conversations, 13, 62–67, 96–97, 118, 126–27, 131–65
Coworkers, 168–71, 183
Creativity, 54, 60, 87–93, 101–2, 115, 139, 158–63, 176

**D**

Dalton, Dr. Jonathan, 83
Dating, 156–59
Demands, releasing, 8, 11, 36–37, 53–58
Depression, 38, 54, 56–57, 62, 76, 92, 104, 106, 116
Diagnosis, 8–9, 57, 67, 110–14, 142–44, 168–69, 182
Dialectical behavior therapy (DBT), 106
Difficult emotions, 74–75, 86–87, 128–29, 162–63
*Disability & Society*, 132
Discrimination, 94, 111, 150, 156
Diversity, 67, 106–11, 118, 133, 139, 152, 163–65, 178–79

**E**

Emotional awareness, 22, 53, 72–80
Emotional clutter, 60–61, 72–73, 98, 173
Emotional intimacy, 162–63
Emotional regulation, 80–91, 100–103, 106–7
Emotional self-care, 9, 22, 53–91, 100–107, 128–29, 162–63
Empathy, 66–69, 112, 132–33, 136
Events, documenting, 18, 85, 172, 174–75
Executive functioning, 15, 23, 38, 44–45, 50–61, 104–5, 114, 167, 184–88
Eye contact, 10, 66, 97, 142, 158, 160–63, 177

**F**

Fatigue, 26–27, 50–51, 55–58, 114, 128, 173
Faux regulation, 165
Fight-or-flight responses, 26–28, 150
*Five Love Languages: How to Express Heartfelt Commitment to Your Mate*, 154
Food challenges, 44–45, 50–52
Foods, safe, 24, 34–35, 50–52
Freeze-fawn mode, 26–28, 140, 151
Friendships, 131, 149–50. *See also* Relationships
*Frontiers in Psychology*, 132
Functioning labels, 96

**G**

Gadsby, Hannah, 72
Gender, 13, 69, 93, 111, 146, 153, 156
Goals, 13, 20, 45, 168–69, 184–85
Goldilocks zone, 181
Gos, Wes, 121
Gottman, Dr. John, 165
Gratitude, 9, 61, 76–77, 125
Gray thinking, 116–17, 122
Green flags, 108, 149
Grief, 114
Grounding techniques, 27, 53, 68–69, 86–89, 100–103, 128–29, 158–61
Gut health, 34–35, 52, 129

**H**

Health care team, 17, 104–11
Healthy relationships, 11, 149–51. *See also* Relationships
Houser, Dr. Mel, 35
Hygiene, 23, 44–52
Hyper-empathy, 68–69
Hyperfocus, 173, 186–87

**I**

Identity board, 115. *See also* Autistic identity
Inertia, 188
Interests, 54–57, 68–69, 93–103, 115, 131, 137, 155–57, 167, 187–88
Internal Family Systems (IFS), 106
Interoception, 14, 18–19, 44–49, 80
Intimacy, 160–63
Isolation, 57, 112, 130, 166

**J**

Job interviews, 83, 176–77
Jobs, Steve, 102–3
Journals, 17–18, 75, 81, 91

**L**

LGBTQIA+ rights, 69
Literacy, 22, 53, 72–79, 119, 139
Love languages, 154–55

**M**

Masking, 10, 14–15, 56–63, 78–79, 95–97, 115, 144–45, 153, 166–71, 177

Meltdowns, 15, 20–21, 56, 67, 100, 112

Mental self-care, 9, 22, 92–129

Mentors, 22, 65, 171, 177, 180

*Metaphilosophy*, 138

Milton, Dr. Damian, 132

Mindfulness, 17, 22, 34–41, 68–69, 80–91, 106–7, 122–29, 173, 186–87

Mindset, 112–15

Monteiro, Dr. Marilyn, 140

Movement, prioritizing, 15, 18–19, 23–37, 87–88, 98–100, 158–59

Muscle tension, 17, 32–33, 129

Music, 39, 55, 75, 87–91, 100, 139, 161, 181

**N**

Neurodivergent identity, 60, 92–95, 107–14, 142–43, 153, 156, 178

Neurotypicals, 10, 70, 94–96, 109, 130–33, 142–48, 162–65, 170–79, 183

Numbness, 27, 56, 90, 128

**O**

Obstacles, 12–15, 50–51. *See also* Challenges

OCD, 92, 104, 106

Overstimulation, 59, 160–61, 181. *See also* Sensory overload

**P**

Painful thoughts, 68–69, 78–79, 88–89, 121–25

Perfectionism, 9, 58, 167, 173

Physical regulation, 24–37

Physical self-care, 9, 21, 23–52

Play, parallel, 137, 155, 158–59, 163

Present moment, 37, 80–91, 100, 123–27, 173. *See also* Mindfulness

Professional self-care, 9, 22, 167–88

Proprioception, 18–19

PTSD, 92, 104, 106

**R**

Racism, 94, 156

Raw spots, 85

Red flags, 108–9, 149, 157

Rejection sensitivity, 150

Relationships
  authentic relationships, 130–43, 153
  friendships, 131, 149–50
  healthy relationships, 11, 149–51
  romantic relationships, 13, 67, 130, 152–66
  sexual relationships, 67, 153, 160–61

Relaxation, 13–21, 24–52, 54–91, 93–129, 131–66, 168–88

Resilience, 13, 22, 53, 72–81, 88–92, 112, 116–29, 173

Rhythmic activities, 29, 55, 59, 98–100, 158–59

Romantic relationships, 13, 67, 130, 152–66

Rudeness, 66, 96, 112

**S**

Safety plan, 20–21

Safety tips, 12–25, 36–37, 62–63, 86–87, 142–50, 156–61

Self-advocacy, 10–19, 53, 62–71, 92, 96, 104–11, 144–45, 174–75

Self-attunement, 14, 22, 49, 57, 78, 81, 150

Self-awareness, 16–19, 22–23, 30–53, 72–91, 146–47

Self-care
  body care/hygiene, 23, 44–52
  emotional self-care, 9, 22, 53–91, 100–107, 128–29, 162–63
  importance of, 9–22
  mental self-care, 9, 22, 92–129
  physical self-care, 9, 21, 23–52
  professional self-care, 9, 22, 167–88
  social self-care, 9, 22, 130–66

Self-compassion, 22, 63, 78–79, 90–95, 112–17

Self-forgiveness, 113

Self-harm alternatives, 86–87, 90

Self-perceptions, 19–20, 94–95, 112–13, 118, 122–23
Self-regulation, 15–22, 24–37, 53, 80–91, 100–107, 128–29
Senses, 15–20, 24–25, 36–37, 160–61
Sensory accommodations, 51, 160–61
Sensory detox, 15, 55–57
Sensory needs, 12–27, 42–48, 62–75, 98–113, 128–30, 149–55, 160–69, 181
Sensory overload, 10, 16–26, 50–59, 80–83, 98–99, 112, 151–65, 181
Sensory preferences, 17–18, 21–22, 42–43, 62, 152
Sensory profile, 15–18, 111, 152, 156
Sensory self-care, 12–22. See also Self-care
Sensory sensitivities, 10, 15–25, 32–39, 46–57, 64–65, 104–9, 154–55, 164–67
"Sensory sickness," 55
Sensory triggers, 15–17, 20–28, 46–47, 66–75, 82–85, 150–51, 158–59, 164–65, 170–87
Sexuality, 153, 160–61, 166
Sexual relationships, 67, 153, 160–61
Shutdowns, 20–21, 26–27, 56
Sleep, improving, 23, 29–33, 37–43, 52, 56, 60–61, 186–87
SMART goals, 184–85
Social self-care, 9, 22, 130–66
Soothing techniques, 10, 17–25, 36–43, 59, 86–89, 102–3, 181
Stereotypes, 13, 66–67, 95, 111, 118, 166, 169
Stigmas, 10, 13, 22, 111, 142
Stimming, 29, 55, 95, 97–100, 161, 181
Stories, changing, 85, 119–21
Stories, sharing, 136, 140–41
Stories, soothing, 59
Stress, managing, 13–21, 24–52, 54–91, 93–129, 131–66, 168–88

T
Task switching, 183
Tension, unwinding, 27, 32–33, 37–39, 129
TENS units, 55, 87
Therapies, 17, 81, 91–92, 104–10, 120–24, 128–29, 165, 169
Thoughts, changing, 116–29, 178–79
Thoughts, mapping, 61, 72–73
Thoughts, painful, 68–69, 78–79, 88–89, 121–25
Thoughts, unrealistic, 116–23
Thunberg, Greta, 102
Tolerance, expanding, 46–47, 86–87, 128–29
Top-down/bottom-up thinking, 178–79
Toxic attachments, 71
Transitions, 24, 47, 144–45, 186–87
Trauma, 15, 49, 92, 104, 106–7, 128–29

U
Unmasking, 15, 53, 62–63, 97, 138–39, 153, 177

V
Vagus nerve, 28, 30–31, 129
Values, identifying, 22, 73, 101, 115, 131
Vestibular system, 18–19
Visualizations, 32–33, 36–45, 60–61, 68–75, 124–25, 174–75, 188
Vitamins/supplements, 52

W
Work accommodations, 22, 110, 167–68, 180–83
Work colleagues, 121, 168–72, 183
Work environments, 167, 174–75, 180–88
Workplace tips, 22, 138–39, 147, 167–88
Worry Period, 84